LUCIFER: PRINCEPS

Lucifer: *Princeps*

PETER GREY · SCARLET IMPRINT · MMXV

Published by Scarlet Imprint
Lucifer Princeps © Peter Grey 2015
Edited, typeset & designed by A. Dimech
Copy edited by Paul Holman

Cover *Satan arousing the rebel angels*
William Blake, 1808; courtesy of V&A Images

ISBN 978-0-9574492-4-4

BM BOX 77777, London WC1N 3XX
SCARLETIMPRINT.COM

For Alkistis, for releasing the light

Contents

A History of Error

It is proper to begin by quoting scripture, in particular the perilous
lines of Isaiah 14:12. This may seem well trodden ground, but all
exegesis starts with Isaiah, and all subsequent errors have, in a sense,
coalesced around this ill-fated pronouncement. The story of Lucifer
can be read as the history of the falsehoods, myths, hopes, hatreds
and dreams that this one line has engendered. It is the centre point
of the web, only made visible by the patient work crafted about it.
The majesty is best conveyed in the King James Version of the Bible,
a masterpiece in its own right, which throngs with satyrs, witches,
sorcerers and dragons. It proclaims:

> How art thou fallen from heaven, O Lucifer, son of the morning!
> how art thou cut down to the ground, which didst weaken the
> nations!

We should take the time to allow these words to resound in our
deepest depths, as they have a weight to them that drops us vertical-
ly into a shrouded stillness. We respond to their magnetic mass. Before we make pronouncement on this doomed figure of fallen light,
we need to sense the gravity of the parabolic descent, and the sense
that we too are part of it. Our inclination is to sympathise with this

romantic figure, to project ourselves down from the heights. It is, in truth, these mysterious words that have exerted their fascination upon us. Having achieved this moment of silent memory, of loss, we can hold this fulcrum steady in the gimbal of our pitching hearts.

The architecture of this vision and vault is buttressed by a history that cannot be sensibly neglected if we are to produce work of any meaningful significance. My task is to examine the context of this evocative slur rather than plucking it from history as a pretty bauble with which to adorn our postmodern motley. I will quote chapter and verse, as it is from the recovery of this myth that we will ultimately draw the form of the ritual which is performed in the subsequent volume *Lucifer: Praxis*. There will be time enough for revelation, but first the hard graft of exegesis is required. Fortunately, there is a wealth of specialist scholarly work available without which the task would be insurmountable. Lest this be considered a fool's coat, made from the offcuts of others' cloth, I will add that this material has not been approached in this way before, and it is tailored for a specific practical purpose. So it begins.

Isaiah is the named author of this crafted curse in what is a great litany of tumbling curses. But, as with Solomon being ascribed authorship of the grimoires, this is a convenient fiction. The chronology of Isaiah spans from the Assyrian occupation to the post-exilic period, encompassing the Babylonian exile, and is delivered as if it were the words of a single prophetic author. There is, however, enough context to date the Lucifer verses; this, at least, seems likely to have been written not by the prophet Isaiah but by Isaiah, son of Amoz, in the mid eighth century BCE.

These lines have been extracted from a highly political text, written in a time of war and disorder, when Israel had been defeated and absorbed into the Assyrian Empire. The context is critical; our author has a radically conservative agenda. His railing against paganism makes the text a repository of heresies. Yet the main thrust of the attack is aimed squarely at the Jewish people, who have turned away from Yahweh, and, in critiquing them, simultaneously appeals to a special inner group of the orthodox:

Hear, O heavens, and give ear, O earth: for the Lord hath spoken,
I have nourished and brought up children, and they have rebelled
against me.

The rebellion takes a specific form: the opposing of divine order,
by acceding to the conquering Assyrians and their vassals. To this
failing is bound the immoral worship of supposedly foreign gods.
Heaped upon the sins of idolatry and sacrifice are attacks on women,
such as the scandalous, adorned beauty of the daughters of Zion,
who are reviled for inciting God's anger. In this regard it is not super-
fluous to quote Isaiah 3:16–24, the exquisite detail of the description
creates a locket that contains, on one face, the hatred of the prophet,
and on the other paradoxically preserves what would have been a
lost vision of beauty. The text is forensic in detail, and precise in
its measuring out of retribution, characteristics that will enable us
to get closer to Lucifer than we could have dared to hope when we
come to consider his fate:

Moreover the Lord saith, Because the daughters of Zion are
haughty, and walk with stretched forth necks and wanton eyes,
walking and mincing as they go, and making a tinkling with their
feet: Therefore the Lord will smite with a scab the crown of the
head of the daughters of Zion, and the Lord will discover their
secret parts. In that day the Lord will take away the bravery of
their tinkling ornaments about their feet, and their cauls, and
their round tires like the moon, The chains, and the bracelets, and
the mufflers, The bonnets, and the ornaments of the legs, and the
headbands, and the tablets, and the earrings, The rings, and nose
jewels, The changeable suits of apparel, and the mantles, and the
wimples, and the crisping pins; The glasses (mirrors), and the fine
linen, and the hoods, and the vails. And it shall come to pass, that
instead of sweet smell there shall be stink; and instead of a girdle
a rent; and instead of well set hair baldness; and instead of a stom-
acher a girding of sackcloth; and burning instead of beauty.

It is women who are so often attacked in scripture as the weak point through which heresy enters, and it is this susceptibility which flourishes into a wilful embrace that becomes a key element of the medieval witch hunts. Adornment, that is, the celebration and enhancement of female sexuality on its own terms, is anathema. The demonisation of carnality – often expressed as the worship of female divinities erroneously glossed as foreign – emerges centuries later in the form of the witch hunting manuals. One reason to study texts such as Isaiah is that the history of ideas is best understood as a churning ocean that dredges up treasures from the depths and deposits them wet and gleaming on the shore before it drags them under again. What is important about this passage is that it highlights how the fate of the transgressors is matched to their supposed crimes, a technique of symmetrical inversion that Isaiah specialises in. An understanding of Lucifer is predicated upon recognising his origins in this process.

Rebellion is the sign of an internal corruption which has led to the fall of the nation to a foreign enemy, in this case Assyria. Elsewhere in Isaiah the enemy is Babylon, as it is in Revelation and other apocalyptic works that do not cite Kittim or Egypt. This sense of an inner enemy weakening the state has been a constant political trope: the motif of a 'fifth column' re-emerged with the witch hunts in the early modern period; more recently we find the argument used in Weimar Germany by the nascent Nazi party, expressed in disproved notions of race and blood; by McCarthy, whose agents fingered Jack Parsons; and currently by the security state whose search is ultimately for ideological heresy.

It is essential to understand the idea of rebellion in its traditional sense, rather than the glamourised or romanticised sense it has come to hold in our culture. The blind imposition of values is one of the most common errors made in reading the past. Rebellion, in particular, has come to be associated with the privileging of a particular pre-verbal emotional state, one that many are heavily invested in. The all too frequent identification with the emotional response to the idea of rebellion prevents us reading history as it was written.

We cannot begin to read the past without first acknowledging that these modern prejudices lead us to overwrite the past, or construct histories that flatter us. My aim is to be effective in sorcery, rather than be ensorcelled. Rebellion has become a marketing device designed to exploit the developmental stage of sexual awakening and differentiation in modern teenagers, who have no formal initiation ritual into adulthood. It is part of a deliberate strategy to create consumers, subverting the drives of social and sexual dissatisfaction by channelling them into brand loyalty and consumption, rather than questioning the values of the corporate state. It avoids the crisis of initiation to keep the population dependent and uncertain in an extended 'kidulthood,' whilst simultaneously breaking social cohesion in favour of the individual – by which is meant the individual as production/consumption unit rather than as sovereign. Rebellion is therefore employed as a key element in commodification. 'Individuals' are simultaneously hypersexualised and de-eroticised. Marcuse wrote eloquently on this, and it is not necessary to embrace his entire Marxist theology to utilise such incisive tools of critique. Put simply, most modern rebellion is not rebellion at all; neither is it harmless: it is actively beneficial to the corporate culture and values it purports to reject. The rebel is rendered impotent by their consumption, whether of pornography or possessions, caught by their own reflection from breaking free into the possibilities of experiences not mediated by constant reference to the screen ideal. Rebellion has, through these and other methods, been very neatly transformed into a tool that creates self-slavery.

In traditional societies, rebellion is understood in a very different sense: namely, opposition to the cosmic order defined by the gods and flowing down through all social relationships. It is a potentially catastrophic event on every plane. We will examine this further when we discuss the antecedents of Isaiah and the coded records of stellar events in our mythic heritage. Rebellion is not a posture of that modern invention of affluence, 'the teenager,' but a crisis that threatens the cosmic fabric.

In Isaiah, the inner corruption of the Jewish people is divined by the prophet, despite their outward demonstrations of piety; a pernicious idea that opens the way for anyone to be accused of heresy, irrespective of their deeds. It is the impossible hunt for purity that societies often embark upon in moments of duress, and one which demands an enemy be found, invented or rebaptised.

In Isaiah 1:13–15, Yahweh berates his people:

> Bring no more vain oblations; incense is an abomination unto me; the new moons and sabbaths, the calling of assemblies, I cannot away with; it is iniquity, even the solemn meeting. Your new moons and your appointed feasts my soul hateth: they are a trouble unto me; I am weary to bear them. And when ye spread forth your hands, I will hide mine eyes from you: yea, when ye make many prayers, I will not hear: your hands are full of blood.

The turning 'backwards' to the trappings of paganism is ultimately proposed as the only explanation as to why their almighty god has abandoned them. Yahweh represents the legitimate cosmic and political order, whose power cascades down into king, priesthood, state and designates woman as the (sexual) property of man. Witchcraft, and the figure of Lucifer, is seen as standing in opposition to this hierarchy.

The appeal to an earlier state of purity is common in apocalyptic literature. So, too, is the condemnation of seemingly virtuous acts as containing some hidden deviance or heretical inflection.[1] As well as being an exoteric method of spreading religious terror, practitioners can exploit this deviant potential in every orthodoxy to invert, or return, the virtue of prayer and ritual in clandestine fashion.

The verses of Isaiah 1:13–15 are a superstitious and magical reaction to a state of interminable crisis and failure. The expectation is that a new golden age of justice will occur after a period of tribulation, but only if the proper rules, dictated from on high, are strictly observed. At times the transformation is said to be the result of the intercession of a Messiah; see, for example, Isaiah 7:14, 9:6. The later sword-tongued Christ of Revelation 1:16, who engages in a combat with a dragon or monster, is perhaps inherited from Isaiah, with Jerusalem as the site of manifest destiny and Babylon as the dragonish enemy. The combat myth is a theme in Canaanite mythology which has clearly influenced both the Old and New Testaments, and though of tangential interest, is not the central theme of our study.[2] Its connections with the development of the 'Son of Man' iconography are a highly contested area of scholarship that we must leave to one side.

What I must necessarily do is define 'apocalypse,' and here, like many scholars in the field, by deferring to J. J. Collins. His definition, given in *The Encyclopedia of Apocalypticism*, is this:

> 'Apocalypse' is a genre of revelatory literature with a narrative
> framework in which a revelation is mediated by an otherworldly
> being to a human recipient, disclosing a transcendent reality
> which is both temporal, in so far as it envisages eschatological
> salvation, and spatial in so far as it involves another, supernatural
> world.

The sources upon which this definition is built are Enoch, Daniel, 4 Ezra, Revelation and 2 Baruch. What Collins' definition lacks is that salvation is most often envisaged for a select group of people, though that does not imply that apocalypticism is the preserve of marginal groups. It engulfs whole cultures as often as it produces the seeming aberration of a Jonestown or Heaven's Gate.

The apocalyptic myth structure can indeed be read in movements as diverse as Marxism, Capitalism, Rosicrucianism, Wahhabi Islam and the New Age. It is worth being familiar with this myth and its variants, as it undergoes spasmodic resurgences and has returned with a vengeance in our war torn times. On the grand stage it seems inevitable that Islam will be used for such an end in our century, but as luxury becomes scarcity, it is inevitable that many others will also find themselves demonised.

Often the idea of apocalypse is ascribed solely to the Judeo-Christian tradition, a troubling legacy that can therefore be safely excluded from our consideration whether as secular, or pagan, moderns. Contrary to this, the mytheme of apocalypse is one of the fundamental elements of the human story. It cannot be traced and confined to the Qumran community or its Zoroastrian precursors, though these must be accounted for if we are to understand Christianity in general and Revelation in particular. Apocalypse, as a myth, has been dated to the Paleolithic in the monumental work of E.J. Michael Witzel.[3] He has utilised the tools of comparative linguistics, genetic data and archaeological evidence to unearth the ur-tales and demonstrated how they have endured throughout the common history of humanity and been forged into a single narrative. This remarkable persistence can be attributed, in part, to the story arising from, and being tethered to, our lifecycle. Thus, if we are to remove the idea of apocalypse, we effectively remove both the initial achievement of consciousness and our inevitable death from the script. Yet these two events are insoluble, our end is found in our beginning. Arguing for a truncated narrative reveals the screens that we have erected to preserve us from the moment of excarnation; it is a thoroughly modern conceit. In apocalypse denial, the spark of life itself is lost, as Lucifer, who represents the promise of the continuity of consciousness, is snuffed out.

Formulation of the Curse

By the time Lucifer enters the fray there has been a litany of rape and
murder as the Lord sets the enemies of Babylon to fall upon her for
the sake of her sins. There is benefit in reading all of Isaiah for its vir-
ulent attacks on groves and statues and offerings and necromancy,
to take in the panorama of destruction wrought in the wrathful fate
of the surrounding nations as they are cursed to ruins, abandoned to
satyrs, dragons and screech owls. Isaiah is no Shakespeare, the analo-
gy biblical scholars like to apply to the book, conveniently forgetting
that it is the work of many hands. The comparison is disingenuous
at best, and part of the whitewashing of the Old Testament to make
it palatable to a modern audience rather than confronting what it
is: a rabidly nationalist history of genocide and hatred. Hence, it
is tempting to become reactive, to indiscriminantly lionise Isaiah's
opponents. But we should remember that Isaiah is still a skilfully
constructed text with precise language and deliberate allusions.
Isaiah consistently employs the formula of reversal, that is, the curse.
The prophecies are not idle threats, they have intent. As with the
invective directed against the daughters of Zion, they are morally
tailored to the ruin of their enemies and are thus highly revealing.
This is not empty parody, this is magical war to restore the balance
of the heavens in the affairs of men. It is intentional malefica of the

9

kind more often ascribed to witches, and traditionally the power of poets.

The lines following Isaiah 14:12, which opened the previous chapter, detail Lucifer's crime. I will examine them in more depth as the study proceeds; but it is important, at this stage, to provide an overview of his fall from grace:

> For thou hast said in thine heart, I will ascend into heaven, I will exalt my throne above the stars of God: I will sit also upon the mount of the congregation, in the sides of the north: I will ascend above the heights of the clouds; I will be like the most High.

Lucifer is styled as an upstart who seeks to set his own throne in the place of Yahweh. This is not overthrowing order, it is an attempt at achieving parity with the divine. Apotheosis, the elevation to the status of a god, is the aim. This suggests a connection to a deeper strata of meaning, of an antecedent myth or myths. Lucifer's fate is then pronounced; and it is here that further vital details are given:

> Yet thou shalt be brought down to hell, to the sides of the pit. They that see thee shall narrowly look upon thee, and consider thee, saying, Is this the man that made the earth to tremble, that did shake kingdoms; That made the world as a wilderness, and destroyed the cities thereof; that opened not the house of his prisoners? All the kings of the nations, even all of them, lie in glory, every one in his own house. But thou art cast out of thy grave like an abominable branch, and as the raiment of those that are slain, thrust through with a sword, that go down to the stones of the pit; as a carcase trodden under feet. Thou shalt not be joined with them in burial, because thou hast destroyed thy land, and slain thy people: the seed of evildoers shall never be renowned. Prepare slaughter for his children for the iniquity of their fathers; that they do not rise, nor possess the land, nor fill the face of the world with cities.

He is cast out of his grave, damned to be a wandering ghost, an exile who will be nameless and not garner the renown due to the Mighty Dead. 'Branch' is here used in the metaphorical sense of bloodline. There is also a wordplay: the root of branch is *nṣr* meaning to guard, keep, watch; which is the role of the king who, in breaking with the limits of his duty, has become abominable. The contrasting ideas are deliberately set against each other.

Isaiah extends the curse to the children of Lucifer, who are stained with their father's sin, a motif I will return to when considering the fate of the Nephilim. But these verses are still scant remarks, not a developed cosmology. We have the sense that Isaiah has revealed and then failed to pursue its narrative; the reason for our misgivings is that these texts presuppose a cultural koiné, a shared mythic language. In order to make sense of Lucifer, beyond rebel posturing, this language must be mastered, for without it there are only the sweeping clouds of grand speculative misunderstandings. The purpose of this study is therefore to reorient the occult tradition within this koiné, in order to engage in meaningful ritual actions that are rooted in a shared ancestry.

It may come as a surprise to those drawn to Lucifer, who seek to escape the limits that monotheism imposes, but my council is not to turn aside from, but to confront, our Judeo-Christian heritage. The Bible is the essential companion to this work. I have included full quotations of the necessary texts so as not to disrupt the narrative flow, additional citations are included for those who wish to pursue their exegetic inquiry further. The Bible has, like a slow moving glacier, not just enveloped, but brought the wreckage of the mountain tops with it, though only the hardest stones have endured, being ground smooth or fissured into grit that slips through our fingers, seemingly unable to impart meaning. But the magician and witch work with the dirt, knowing that it has retained its virtue. We find tradition even here, sifted patiently from the melt water of tottering seracs. The bright inheritance is here; through fast flowing rivers it is trapped in the fleeces which glitter with fragments of timeless gold. In patiently prospecting for the traditions which antecede both Judaism and Christianity the ever bright light emerges.

At this juncture I must pause, I have deliberately misled you. The quote which names Lucifer is founded on an error in translation, a virus of light. When we read the text in the original form our cherished Lucifer vanishes like a cat in a coal cellar.

The Dawn Breakers

Lucifer does not exist until the stroke of a pen in 382 CE. The genealogy is straightforward to plot. First, the apparent name given in Isaiah 14:12 is not Lucifer, but Hêlēl Ben Šaḥar; this is transformed in the Septuagint, the Greek translation of the Hebrew Bible, into Ἐωσφόρος (Heōsphóros): Dawn bringer. This is the specific Greek term for the god of the planet Venus when it rises. There is no ambiguity in its astral identification as the morning star. In Greek mythology, Heōsphóros was twinned with Hesperos; they are respectively morning and evening star. Even in identifying these as gods of the star, the planet Venus herself remained that of the love goddess Aphrodite, a distinction which needs to be made.

The Septuagint, with its rendition of Heōsphóros, was not, however, used as the basis for the Latin Vulgate, which replaced the earlier translations in circulation, collectively known as the Vetus Latina. The Latin Vulgate was the work of St Jerome in a project which commenced in 382 CE, and became the standard text in the Western Catholic Church for the next 1000 years. Instead of using the Greek Septuagint, Jerome went to the Hebrew texts themselves, and thence made the fatal translation 'Lucifer.' This is derived from the Latin *lucem ferre*, light bearer. Clearly this differs from the Greek, 'dawn bringer,' although it has the same essential meaning, that of

Venus, the morning star. It is only when the Latin Lucifer is translated back into Greek that it becomes φωσφόρος (Phōsphóros). Evidently, dawn-bringer is not a term that can be used interchangeably with phosphoros, which has the more general meaning of 'light-bringing,' and is applied to many gods and goddesses, such as torch-bearing Hecate. It does not identify the source or the character of the light. Though 'phosphoros' can be applied as an epithet to Lucifer, it would be more accurate to specify 'heosphoros.' The mystery of Lucifer is explicitly concerned with the light of dawn, and its attendant qualities – the reddening of the sky and the magical properties of the dew, an oft forgotten elixir.

Having clarified the confusion in translation, another tool of analysis can be applied: when a word or phrase is used in the Bible it is often taken to deliberately reference other uses of it, seeded throughout the entire text – this is concordance, an important tool of exegesis, though unless applied with discretion it can lead into error. Concordance can be thought of in the same manner as the Beat concept of the cut-up. Each fragment contains a connection to the original use, though now positioned in relation to another word, which creates a third meaning. The word contains the entirety of its history, associations and powers intact. In the example of the Beats, the combinations are random (though the texts are selected), and then interrogated for new, revealed meanings. In the Bible the connections are seen as deliberate, the work of God, creating a complex web of interrelated mythemes and motifs. It is a magical procedure, and comparable to the creation of talismans, which are wrought through the understanding and willed combination of elements. These, for the natural magician, belong to a chain of sympathies extending from the chthonic to the celestial. If we are to apprehend Lucifer then it is necessary to pursue him in every instance that his name occurs; this process will equip us with his signature.

Every Bible contains a concordance; the entries for Lucifer are mercifully brief, yet we can expand this somewhat and note that luciferum is used in the Vulgate to mean the morning star in Psalm 109:3 (Psalm 110 in the KJV), *Tecum principium in die virtutis tuae in splendoribus sanctorum: ex utero, ante luciferum, genui te.* Which is rendered in the KJV as, 'Thy people shall be willing in the day of thy power, in the beauties of holiness from the womb of the morning: thou hast the dew of thy youth.'

Luciferum has quietly become 'morning,' not morning star. It is an adjective, not a proper name, and hence not capitalised. What we should be aware of is the archaic language of this Davidic text, particulary in the kingship formula: womb of the morning, dew of thy youth.[1] This tells of the resurrection of the king through the goddess, a critical idea in this study. Psalm 110 is used extensively in the New Testament, especially in Hebrews, to support the messianic claims of Jesus. In doing so it preserves the earlier stratum of ritual practice that we seek to cleave to, and the exact words of the ritual formula.

Luciferum appears again in Job 38, with the sense of 'shining,' although in this instance it is an inaccurate gloss for Mazzaroth (the Zodiac). Note that in neither instance is it used in a pejorative or mocking way.

However, the Latin Vulgate has sown confusion with 2 Peter 1:19 where *lucifer* is equated with Christ, *Et habemus firmiorem propheticum sermonem: cui benefacitis attendentes quasi lucernae lucenti in caliginoso donec dies elucescat, et lucifer oriatur in cordibus vestris.* Whereas in the KJV *lucifer* is given as 'day star'; the Latin translates as 'We have also a more sure word of prophecy; whereunto ye do well that ye take heed, as unto a light that shineth in a dark place, until the day dawn, and lucifer arises in your hearts.'

The passage does not use 'lucifer' as a noun. Rather, Christ is characterised as like the morning star, that is, as *like* lucifer but not *as* Lucifer, the divine personage or entity. There are clearly equivalences between these two figures, which we will explore as our exegesis progresses. Yet this is not some esoteric revelation, it is rather that they share the common cultural koiné of Ancient Near Eastern kingship. Nor is this the sole occurrence where Christ is described in terms of the morning star; there are three further instances in the Vulgate which use another term: *stella matutina*. These are Ecclesiasticus 50:6, 'He was as the morning starre in the midst of a cloud: and as the moone at the full'; the oblique Revelation 2:28, 'And I will give him the morning star'; and lastly, the unequivocal Revelation 22:16, 'I Jesus have sent mine angel to testify unto you these things in the churches. I am the root and the offspring of David, and the bright and morning star.'

John in Revelation is, no doubt, repeating the image of 2 Peter 1:19 given earlier. The *stella matutina* is an apt image for the new dawn of Christ the King, which nonetheless drew heavily from existent Semitic myths.

Some pagan writers[2] have proposed that this is part of the 'stealing' of Venus and in doing so played its part in the demonisation of the goddess. I find this too simplistic a reading; the extant complex of ideas around the morning star, or dawn light, refer to kingship and should not be seen exclusively as an attack on the goddess: a quite modern interpretation betraying contemporary neopagan concerns. The mystery we are concerned with is that of the light which emerges from the darkness of the grave and womb. Such is the essential mystery of Lucifer which has been so long occluded.

Evangelical Christians have also wrestled with the use of Lucifer in scripture and come to a typically tortured conclusion. Scripture makes it impossible for them to deny that Christ is the morning star, whilst it is also evident from Isaiah that Lucifer is too. They therefore accept that Christ is the morning star, due to the New Testament sources we have quoted, but then go on to propose that the Lucifer of Isaiah in the Old Testament must be the false morning star in that he is fallen in his attempt to usurp the position of God. This draws on the New Testament idea of the enemy disguised as an angel of light, which will flourish in medieval demonology, and the role and symbolism of Antichrist in Revelation. The Evangelicals are aware of the potential error in equating Lucifer with Christ, and the subsequent generation of a gnostic heresy from confounding Redeemer and Enemy. Lucifer in Isaiah is – for the Evangelicals – Satan, the dragon, the Devil. Attempts to stray from the KJV, and propose 'day star' or 'morning star' as alternative translations, are styled as part of a creeping tide of modernism (no doubt satanically

inspired) that seeks to remove the Devil from scripture. Their cate-
chism echoes Baudelaire: the finest trick of the devil is to persuade
you that he doesn't exist, though no doubt they prefer to advocate
the bowdlerised version of C.S. Lewis.

Another cause of confusion occurs in Hebrews, the New Testament text that, as previously shown, relies so heavily on Psalm 110.
Here Jesus is described no less than five times as 'exalted to the right
hand of God,' an image perilously close to Isaiah 14:13, where Lucifer
is seated upon the mount of the congregation. As both are kings they
are identically clothed. Christ appeals for legitimacy to the archaic
symbols of the Royal House of David, whereas Lucifer is an improper
ruler but still bears the same insignia. Both draw on the same cultural conventions of divine kingship.

The feared error of mistaking Lucifer for Christ is exactly what we
find in some modern esoteric interpretations. At times, the similitude is presented as an esoteric Christianity; at others, as a core
component within certain streams of modern traditional witchcraft.
Such theories draw heavily on modern angelic speculation – more
proto-New Age than historically derived.[3] Deeming Christ as Lucifer
and Lucifer as Christ is a logical nonsense, rooted in a 19th century
conception of a universal religion, as mooted by the Theosophists.
Other notable attempts to solve the Christ-Lucifer antipathy are to
be found in Thelema and The Process Church of the Final Judgment
– again, in origin, theosophically inspired. My position on the
matter is clear: Lucifer is not Christ, as a careful reading of scripture
demonstrates. The confusion is due to a shared metaphor, or more
accurately, epithet, that references an undergirding unity: kingship.

The error has occured because of the misuse of concordance as a
tool of exegesis. In comparing the use of phrases and words to draw
equivalences, none of the theories cited above distinguish between
the capitalised name Lucifer, as introduced by St Jerome, and the
New Testament use of the uncapitalised morning star as a metaphor for Christ. Neither do they take account of the context of the
passages. By combining and identifying the figures of Lucifer and
Christ, such readings inevitably go on to render Satan anathema.

The impossibility of such a reading will be addressed in due course, as both scripture and the historical record unequivocally show that Lucifer and Satan are bound to one another. Language is a slippery thing, and we must be careful, in our eagerness to decipher meaning, that we do not repeat such avoidable errors.

The Shining One

Our exegesis now proceeds apace: who is it that Isaiah invokes, if not a discrete entity going by the name of Lucifer? The text identifies a specific character, given the title *hêlēl ben šaḥar*, a physical man who will be eaten by maggots and worms. Hêlēl Ben Šaḥar is not a personal name, but a title for the king of Babylon, the target of Isaiah's wrath. He is neither errant angel nor divinity, let alone the ruler of the underworld. The exact identity of the king remains disputed, although context makes it likely to be the Assyrian, Sargon II, who ruled from 722 to 705 BCE and conquered all of Israel.

Sargon II is mentioned in Isaiah 20:1 in relation to the subjugation of Ashdod in 711 BCE, which completed his conquest of Israel. This reference masks the fact that he was one of the great monarchs of the ancient Orient.[1] At this point I should add further salient biographic details:[2] Sargon (Šarru-kīnu in Assyrian) means 'the true King.' Sargon I (Šargani-šar-ali), a ruler who antedated him by some two thousand years, provided him with a mythical pedigree. Šargani means 'a god has established himself as king,'[3] which is indicative of the divine nature of kingship in the ancient world. Sargon's appeal to the ancient model, and the absence of intermediary monarchs in his line, is noteworthy; it adds weight to the theory that he usurped the throne of his half-brother Šalmaneser V (726–722 BCE), and the likelihood that he was the son of a concubine of Tiglath-Pileser III (745–727 BCE). He was supported in power by the priestly elite. Such details would be grist to Isaiah's mill. Sargon I's myth is of crucial importance:[4] he is birthed in secret by a low-born woman, placed in a reed basket[5] and raised by the royal gardener who discovers him. He goes on to become the lover of the goddess Ištar. In imitation of Sargon I, Sargon set up a stele in Cyprus, having crossed the sea of the setting sun. This is an important aside, as Cyprus is the island of the love goddess, the connection between Aphrodite and Inanna/Ištar explicit. Without the goddess there is no kingship.

Sargon engaged in war every year of his reign until his death at the hands of Ešpai, a Kimmerian tribal leader. His conquests had not required him to take to the field in every combat; such a risk would have been unacceptable. Sidney Smith gives this verdict on the event:

> The unprecedented death on the battlefield of the Assyrian king must have struck the newly conquered peoples with seismic force, and its reverberations can be heard in the Old Testament.[6]

This refers to Isaiah. The death of Sargon is the climactic moment for the Assyrian Empire. No longer will edicts be issued such as the one he gave to the people of Anatolia, 'Now eat your bread, and drink your water under the shadow of the king my lord, and be glad!'[7] The symbol of the shadow used here will return to haunt us. The death of Sargon was deftly turned in Isaiah to evidence the supremacy of Yahweh.

Sargon provides the historical figure behind Isaiah's polemic, but this is the beginning and not the end of the matter. Sargon has a mythic dimension based upon an ancient conception of kingship common across the Near East which even during the Assyrian Empire harked back to Sumer for its legitimacy. The figure of Sargon cannot provide the ultimate answer to our search for the identity of Lucifer; Isaiah yields no easy answers for it is a multivalent narrative. Let us now return to the font of the error and seek to rectify it by examining the original words which anointed the brow of Lucifer. The text is more accurately rendered:

> How art thou fallen from heaven, Hêlēl Ben Šaḥar! How art thou cut down to the ground, which didst weaken the nations!

Neither his fate, nor his crime, are unique; similar language is used by Jesus in Matthew 11:23, where he castigates a series of unrepentant cities. It is the repetition of a formula: a curse.

> And thou, Capernaum, which art exalted unto heaven, shalt be brought down to hell: for if the mighty works, which have been done in thee, had been done in Sodom, it would have remained until this day.

It is also present in Ezekiel 28:17, in the attack on the King of Tyre:

> Thine heart was lifted up because of thy beauty, thou hast corrupted thy wisdom by reason of thy brightness: I will cast thee to the ground, I will lay thee before kings, that they may behold thee.

These examples do not exhaust a vein that striates the living rock of the Old and New Testaments, from the alpha to the omega, from Genesis to Revelation. It is necessary, therefore, to first gain insight into the title, *hêlēl ben šaḥar*, which Isaiah applies to the king of Babylon, in order to establish its consequence. Otherwise Isaiah would read 'Oh Sargon, how fallen art thou,' and our investigation would be concluded. The title is commonly translated as 'Helel, Son of Dawn,' which is in accord with the idea conveyed by the Septuaguint's Heōsphóros and the Vulgate's Lucifer.[8] The logical approach is thus to find a corresponding myth, of a Son of Dawn who rises and is struck down, and with whom Sargon has been equated. However, the search for such a myth has proved more problematic than many had initially hoped.

A Babylonian original was proposed by the early and influential biblical scholar Hermann Gunkel,[9] but no extant myth fits without violence being done to either story. Ištar, Enlil and Gilgameš have been cited, but the Babylonian theses have now been abandoned by the majority of academics. Where could the search then lead? Canaanite religion seemed the next most likely place for such cultural borrowing, with a pantheon which included El, Baal, Ašerah, Mot and Yam, figures all glimpsed in scriptural asides. Yet no significant evidence was available for scrutiny until the discovery of the Ugaritic texts in the 1920s, with further discoveries through to the 1970s, in what is now Syria. Written in alphabetic cuneiform, the texts shed light on many previously elusive terms found in the Old Testament and as a result are considered essential by modern biblical scholars. The Psalms, in particular, have been shown to rely heavily on Canaanite texts, and much of the identity of Yahweh is now accepted to have been created out of the fabric of the Canaanite El. Any texts that consider Hêlēl Ben Šaḥar, written before these discoveries, are therefore found severely wanting.[10]

The initial response of the academy was to relate the Baal texts to Isaiah. One myth in particular was promoted: the Ugaritic tale of Athtar, the god of the morning star taking the throne of Baal. This seemed a congruent solution, especially given the mention in Isaiah of a location for the tale, Mount Zaphon, a site that will concern us in the next chapter. We have found a figure in the landscape, but we should not rush to accept that the Athtar of the Baal texts is our sought after Lucifer on the sole evidence that the myth is located at Zaphon – it being the location given in Isaiah for the fall. Examining the Ugaritic myth a little more closely reveals a major discrepancy. Athtar is not thrown down but, in contrast, acknowledges his inferiority and voluntarily abdicates his station. KTU 1.6 I 63–65 makes this clear:

> Athtar the Strong descends,
> Descends from the throne of the Mightiest Baal,
> And rules over all the great earth.

It has all the appearances of a negotiated settlement, rather than a violent deposition. Athtar does not measure up, the text relates how: 'His feet do not reach the footstool, his head does not reach the top (of the throne)'; a very different fate to that meted out to Hêlêl Ben Šaḥar, who is dramatically cast down. One proposed reading of the text is that it records, in the language of myth, a shift in power from Athtar, an astral deity and warrior god, to that of Baal, a rival warrior god and the patron of the Ugaritic dynasty.

Athtar is, for the most part, translated as 'strong'; a rendition favoured by some modern occultists, who have seized on Athtar as their Ur-Lucifer, whilst ignoring the ostensible fact that he does not fall. Paradoxically, it is Baal who is the rising and dying god. Attempts by modern practitioners to create a Satanically-inflected Canaanite religion on this basis are not anchored in the past, but arise from their modern preoccupations combined with a selective reading of the evidence. The case appears to be built on little more than a footnote in Astour's *Hellenosemitica*, that relates Athtar to the double name, Ngh w Srr, found in the Ugaritic divine list (KTU 1.123:12/RŠ 24.271). Astour gives the translation of these terms as 'brightness' and 'rebellion,' both epithets of a Luciferian nature. Further research, however, reveals that this is disputed; *srr* is more accurately the last night of the lunar month, and both terms refer, not to Venus, but to the Moon.

The text can be read in another way, one rooted in the specific topography of the myth. Athtar is cognate with the Arabic *attari*, irrigated soil, and *atur*, canal or trench; this gives a fuller sense of a god who is equated, not only with the morning star, but also with the morning mist. Athtar, by this methodological approach, is intrinsically related to irrigation-based agriculture, which cannot compete with the inundating rainfall of Baal. It further references the fall in the water table during the early Bronze Age. This explains the conflict between the gods; the reason for the place where the action is set (the rain-shrouded peak of Mount Zaphon); and the subsequent return of Athtar to rulership of the Earth. It describes a culture reliant on rain, not aquifers and ingenuity. In this light, the myth cycle looks very different: it is specific to a place, a people and a time.

The evidence undermines what had once seemed a logical line of enquiry: that Hêlēl Ben Šaḥar was a specific character from the retelling of the Ugaritic Baal cycle. But the idea of kingship and rain-making are not in conflict, in fact quite the opposite is true. Yahweh demonstrates as much, in 1 Kings 18, where he triumphs as rainmaker, and an inglorious massacre is enacted upon the priests of Baal who fail to do so. The chief function of the king is defined by the storm god and his ability to fecundate the land, which is no longer seen as a chthonic power – as exemplified by the serpent and the woman in prehistory – but a celestial role, hammered out in the Bronze and subsequent Iron Age. Yahweh combines the role of supreme creator with all the attributes of the storm; elements that the Bible and biblical scholars have redacted from accounts of rival pantheons, to make them merely personified elemental forces. A careful survey of the cult literature shows them in far more nuanced form than if we rely on the Bible as our sole trusted source. This 'myth of progress' reading is clearly designed to depict paganism as smoothly eclipsed by the superiority of monotheism.

The academy has taken several different approaches in response to the collapse of the Baal cycle theory. Here I should stress that the Ugaritic texts are partial, we only have elements of them and the sources are very early: the middle of the second millennium. Thus, there is no way to discern whether a story of the fall formed part of a later, or even parallel, Canaanite myth structure. Mindful of this, Wildberger[11] has proposed a retelling of a lost story, in which Hêlēl seeks to be enthroned as king of the universe and is cast down by El Elyon. It must be said, however, that there is no proof to support this new, and convenient, tale ever existing in Canaanite mythology. Therefore this, and any similar attempts to reconstruct the myth, must be considered conjecture. William Foxwell Albright, in his *Yahweh and the Gods of Canaan*,[12] is one scholar who goes further, seeing Isaiah as only containing vestigial (Canaanite) myths that have

PRINCEPS

been demythologised to the status of poetic fragments.[13] The denial of myth he proposes seems disingenuous, if not partial. It reveals another problem with the study of biblical literature: that it is often driven by theological and political agendas which seek to emphasise and underplay elements of what is a highly complex story. For some, the idea that the Bible contains pagan mythological motifs remains an abomination.[14]

Holy Mountain

The search for Lucifer must be grounded in place. Though the motive
for rebellion is located in the heart, the deed is enacted, not solely
in the remoteness of the heavens, but simultaneously upon a holy
mountain. Isaiah 14:13 provides more than a backdrop, it plays the
cosmic action out upon a richly storied landscape:

> For thou hast said in thine heart, I will ascend into heaven, I will
> exalt my throne above the stars of God: I will sit also upon the
> mount of the congregation, in the sides of the north:

In the King James Version this is not made apparent. Mount Zaphon
is not named but is referred to by its geographical position, *the North.*
This was the home of Baal.[1] Zaphon – now known as Jebel El-'Aqra,
literally 'the bare mountain' – lies on the Syro-Palestinian border, a
1770 metre dominating limestone peak some 40 kilometres north of
Ras Shamra (Ugarit). This was where the rain-seeded clouds from
the Mediterranean gathered their dove-dark folds.[2]

What is somewhat difficult in the KJV is the full phrase:, 'I will sit
also upon the mount of the congregation, in the sides of the north.'
'Sides' (*yerekah*) can also be translated as furthermost point; inaccessible; or recess. In this passage it refers to the summit of the moun-

tain. This is shown in the verse after next, Isaiah 14:15, 'Yet thou shalt be brought down to hell, to the sides of the pit,' which uses the same word to intensify the contrasting pair of ideas: the highest and lowest. This is far more than a convenient topographic metaphor.

The meaning of the name Zaphon is not easy to adduce. It has been identified with the Hebrew ṣāpâ, to keep watch, deriving from ṣāpan, to conceal or hide; or as the North, the North Wind. It is even suggested as deriving from ṣûp, to swim, or flood. All seem appropriate for the shrouded watchtower that presides over the chaos of the waters.

Zaphon was considered to be the high point of the midday sun in the eastern Mediterranean. As the archetypal mountain in the North, it has the implication of being directly beneath the pole star, and thus of cosmic import as the world axis. A vestigial trace of this is found in Genesis where the disposition of the tribes of Israel are oriented about Zaphon.

The holy mountain housed the cult sanctuary of Baal, built from celestial blue lapis and glittering sliver. The mountain, and its locale, was the site of Baal's battles with Yam (the sea), Mot (death) and Lotan (the seven headed dragon).[3] This is echoed by the description of Yahweh, patterned on the Lord of the Canaanite holy mountain, in Job 26:7-14. Perhaps the passage is another example of a lifted text inserted into the rival religion's scripture. Whether the text is patterned, or purloined, the God of Israel evoked in Job is identical to the Canaanite Baal, sharing motifs of place, powers and opponents:

He stretcheth out the north over the empty place, and hangeth the earth upon nothing. He bindeth up the waters in his thick clouds; and the cloud is not rent under them. He holdeth back the face of his throne, and spreadeth his cloud upon it. He hath compassed the waters with bounds, until the day and night come to an end. The pillars of heaven tremble and are astonished at his reproof. He divideth the sea with his power, and by his understanding he smiteth through the proud. By his spirit he hath garnished the heavens; his hand hath formed the crooked serpent.

Lo, these are parts of his ways: but how little a portion is heard of him? but the thunder of his power who can understand?

Job appears remarkable in providing this vista of the Baal of Zaphon, but it is neither unique nor an aberration. Elsewhere, elements of Baal's holy mountain, Zaphon, have been applied to Mount Zion. Psalm 48:1–2 conflates the two:

Great is the Lord, and greatly to be praised in the city of our God, in the mountain of his holiness. Beautiful for situation, the joy of the whole earth, is mount Zion, on the sides of the north, the city of the great King.

As Clifford[4] remarks, even Mount Sinai, the Old Testament mountain of law-giving, stands in the Canaanite tradition of the cosmic mountain: the primeval mound, the place where god dwelt, the meeting place of heaven and earth where fertilising streams burst forth, and marked the place of battle where god's enemies will ultimately be defeated. Yahweh is not like Baal, who is seasonally defeated by Mot, and therefore the mountain was imagined as an unimpregnable stronghold.

Turning to Ezekiel 1:4, in search of more examples, Zaphon is now revealed to be the source of the vision, again obliquely given in the KJV as 'the north':

And I looked, and, behold, a whirlwind came out of the north, a great cloud, and a fire infolding itself, and a brightness was about it, and out of the midst thereof as the colour of amber, out of the midst of the fire.

The vision that issues from Zaphon can be understood as a thunderstorm, flickering with lightning; a psychedelic vista to be sure, but not one lacking setting. Even positing an entheogenic impetus for the visions (and I do not), does not permit us to escape the actuality that they are founded upon both a physical landscape and an established set of mythic conventions. With this realisation, we can interpret the remainder of Ezekiel's revelation, rather than gloss our ignorance with the suggestion that it must be some kind of 'trip' with which we can free associate. The vision has substance, and it is drawn from the pattern of Assyrian kingship, as Simo Parpola observes:

> In the royal palace, the king lived in a sacred space designed and built after celestial patterns and guarded against the material world by deities and apotropaic figures stationed at its gates and buried in its foundations. Colossal supernatural beings in the shape of a bull, lion, eagle and man, symbolizing the four turning points, guarded its gates. These apotropaic colossi marked the palace as a sacred space and thus may be compared to the four guardians of the divine throne in Ezekiel 1:10 and Revelation 4:7, which later re-emerge as symbols of the four evangelists of the New Testament: Matthew (man), Mark (lion), Luke (bull) and John (eagle).[5]

The accuracy of Parpola is confirmed by the references to scripture he gives. For those unfamiliar with Ezekiel and Revelation I will cite these and additional supporting lines for added context. In Ezekiel, the prophet encounters the guardian cherubim:

> As for the likeness of their faces, they four had the face of a man, and the face of a lion, on the right side: and they four had the face of an ox on the left side; they four also had the face of an eagle.

This is followed by a vision of God as an Assyrian/Mesopotamian king seated in the lapis lazuli palace of Baal.[6] It is the theophany of a storm god, where amber (Greek ἤλεκτρον, *ēlektron*) serves as the generating force of divinity:

> And above the firmament that was over their heads was the likeness of a throne, as the appearance of a sapphire stone: and upon the likeness of the throne was the likeness as the appearance

of a man above upon it. And I saw as the colour of amber, as the appearance of fire round about within it, from the appearance of his loins even upward, and from the appearance of his loins even downward, I saw as it were the appearance of fire, and it had brightness round about. As the appearance of the bow that is in the cloud in the day of rain, so was the appearance of the brightness round about. This was the appearance of the likeness of the glory of the Lord. And when I saw it, I fell upon my face, and I heard a voice of one that spake.

The debt owed to this by Revelation is apparent, see 4:2–10 below:

And immediately I was in the spirit: and, behold, a throne was set in heaven, and one sat on the throne. And he that sat was to look upon like a jasper and a sardine stone: and there was a rainbow round about the throne, in sight like unto an emerald. And round about the throne were four and twenty seats: and upon the seats I saw four and twenty elders sitting, clothed in white raiment; and they had on their heads crowns of gold. And out of the throne proceeded lightnings and thunderings and voices: and there were seven lamps of fire burning before the throne, which are the seven Spirits of God. And before the throne there was a sea of glass like unto crystal: and in the midst of the throne, and round about the throne, were four beasts full of eyes before and behind. And the first beast was like a lion, and the second beast like a calf, and the third beast had a face as a man, and the fourth beast was like a flying eagle.

Zaphon is not only the watchtower, but the place where the god descends; an event which is commemorated in both Jewish and Christian accounts.[7] This location is a mythological nexus, a disputed mountain, a vortex about which not only the clouds swirl, but a host of stories which Isaiah has deliberately summoned. The reason for the conflict that Lucifer is implicated in is becoming more solid: it is a battle for the legitimacy to rule, expressed in the shared symbols of Near Eastern kingship. Isaiah has Sargon challenging Yahweh, the divine ruler, at the site of the holy mountain where his hubris is punished by an ignoble death.

The story of Mount Zaphon does not originate with Isaiah, neither does it perish with him; its significance persists from the Hellenic period into the Roman Empire and beyond. Just as Lucifer is not confined to a single historical event or being, but is a character who evolves over time, it is important to relate the history of the mountain upon which the myth occurs.

Standing on the peak of Zaphon, priests observed the wheel of the heavens above, pinned by the North Star and its twining serpent. They watched the Sun rise in the East, heralded by Venus. Dawn broke the rulership of night. The fiery solar chariot plotted the course of the day to set beyond Cyprus in the West, visible to them across the wine dark sea. Fittingly, it is the island of the love goddess where Venus is seen again, now risen as evening star. Observers traced not only the patterns of star and season and storm, but other messengers that streaked sudden from the heavens, as lightning does. These endured as signs, as visitors, as gods. The star stones and meteorite cults will require interrogation, alongside the other significant pilgrims who came to Zaphon in search of oracles.

The Greeks called Zaphon Mount Kasios, the Hurrians Hazzi. Folk etymology connects this to the Hebrew hzh, to see. It was a vital navigational aid and, as the guardian of its peak was the victor over the monsters of the sea (Typhon/Lotan/Yam/Leviathan); it was appealed to by mariners for safe passage.

The cult of Baal Zaphon/Zeus Kasios spread as far as Egypt through maritime exchange, becoming associated with Horus and his battle with Typhon. The Egyptians named a mountain of their own Kasios, even though it was little more than a sand dune. They dedicated the lake next to it to Typhon, and the mist which formed on its surface at dawn they knew as 'Typhon's breath.'[8] This example shows how magic moves and can be adapted congruently to new environments.

In 300 BCE Seleucus, the (Diadochan) successor of Alexander

founded a city after climbing the peak to sacrifice at dawn. An eagle took part of the sacrifice and where it fell the city was built. Thunderbolt struck coins commemorated the event; the god had spoken.

Seleucus was not the last illustrious visitor to the summit. No less than three Roman Emperors felt obliged to make pilgrimage and seek the blessing of the divinity they called Zeus Kasios. Trajan was present in the winter of 114–115 CE; he was not alone, but was accompanied by Hadrian, who composed these lines to Zeus Kasios in hope of success in their military campaign:

> Trajan, son of Aeneas, has dedicated this gift to Zeus Kasios – the ruler of men to the ruler of the immortals. that same mortal now deposits two deftly wrought silver cups and a horn adorned with glittering gold, taken from an aurochs bison. All these things have been chosen with care from his earlier spoils seized when he laid waste the dacians with his lance. but you, lord of the dark clouds, we beseech you to grant him the power to bring this coming parthian war to a successful end, so that your heart may be twice warmed by the sight of twin sets of spoils, with those of the Parthians soon to be set alongside those of the Dacians.

There is clearly continuity of practice here, as wild ox horns were the correct ancient offering. The ox horns represent the furthest reaches of sunrise and sunset, visible from the summit.[9] The ox is also one of the animal forms and mounts of the storm god.

Trajan was subsequently saved from an earthquake, which he attributed to the direct intervention of Zeus Kasios, and they were indeed triumphant in their war. Coins struck after this event show a four-posted shrine surmounted with an eagle (the symbol of Zeus) and bearing the unequivocal legend 'Zeus Kasios.' The shrine contains a further element that appears, at first glance, to be an enigmatic baetyl, a holy stone, a meteorite. This roughly conical omphaloid stone displays a recess or sanctuary beneath the summit and could be considered a fallen celestial form of the mountain itself. We cannot ascertain that a thunder stone was represented on the coins, however appropriate it may seem, and however prevalent the cults to holy stones in the region.[10] It seems most likely that it is the mountain itself, rather than, for example, a stone like that of Cybele (also depicted on coins in the period).

Hadrian returned in 130 CE to climb the mountain and witness the epiphanic sunrise. The importance of the timing is given by Ammianus Marcellinus (*Ammianus* 22.14.4), who relates that the Sun is seen here before anywhere else in the world, at the moment of the second cock crow.[11] The Syrian emperor Elagabal (203–222 CE) had similar coins cast to those of Trajan, depicting a mysterious stone beneath a canopy. His have an additional detail: beneath the eagle and in the triangular recess of the roof that surmounts the stone is a star cradled in a lunar crescent. Yet this is a different baetyl altogether, that of El Gabal, the god of the mountain and invincible sun god of Emesa. On the worn coins we can still make out the defining characteristic of this divine stone: a depression in the shape of the Sun. Such a cult of the god of the high places, the worship of a meteorite, the flamboyant and sacrilegious actions of Elagabalus were too much for even Rome to bear and lead to his murder. It is arguable that the biography of Elagabalus has retrospectively informed ideas of Lucifer as errant monarch. What we can state for certain is that the cult of Sol Invictus Elagabal endured in the Empire until its collapse, with the Christian cult preserving not only his birthday for their own Saviour but other salient features.

In 363 CE our final illustrious pilgrim made his trek: Julian, the Apostate, the last pagan emperor. In the dawn light of Spring he too encountered Zeus Kasios on the summit. The theophany of the bearded genius of the mountain peak was for Julian transformative; but with the victory of Christianity, the pilgrimages ceased and the sanctuary was destroyed, the peak now the home of stylites. By the time we reach a Christian Europe all such spirit encounters are deemed to be Faustian and can have only one protagonist.

The cults made to fallen stones were a feature of the religious life of the ancient world. Such cults were also to be found in the regions contiguous with Mount Zaphon and its genius. But in the case of

Lucifer, his association with meteorites must be considered as an exegetic development from the scriptural notion of the fall found in Isaiah, Genesis and Revelation. The symbol of the meteorite must therefore be considered apposite, though not foundational. There is a poetic harmony which is for practitioners rather than historians, to pursue. I would argue that the reconquest of such images forms an important aspect of working with Lucifer. Sky iron bestowed by the heavens has weighted magical significance; it recalls the gift of metallurgy that Lucifer brings; it is a living, divine metal that can be wrought with artifice into new forms. Accepting the valency of the meteorite image does not chain us to the trajectory of failed flight, but can be witnessed as the bright renewal of promise, providential drops fallen from the starry forge that bore us.

Lucifer does not remain in the Near East, and, as he translates to Europe, we find further points of congruence: holy mountains, blasted heaths and the mysterious dwelling places of our own ancestors. As we pursue Lucifer, our eyes will continue to be lifted to regard the distant peak upon which our bare feet must tread.

Denied access to Mount Zaphon by war, we should not despair of having such an epiphany. We can take these mythic events and transpose them into our own sacred landscape, understanding that this axis, this height where spirit and destiny makes itself known is not bound to one locale, but that the genius loci awaits us, if we only dare to seek it out at the gates of dawn, dusk, midday and midnight, as well as those that open in the transit of the year.

Scorched Heavens, Burned Earth

The fall of Lucifer is not a unique mythic event. His fate is mirrored in a plethora of figures in the Ugaritic, Greek and Mesopotamian traditions, whose legends are marked by certain common elements: doomed flight, the bringing of the fire of knowledge, and transgressing the limits of divine power. Notable amongst these figures are Icarus, Etana, Athtar, Gilgameš, Prometheus, Phaëthon and Bellerophon. All are worthy of study. The biblical sources are supplemented by the great storehouse of myth. The sparsity of the references, in Isaiah in particular and scripture in general, is fleshed and feathered out with borrowings from the common cultural inheritance.

Having acknowledged the breadth and depth of possible influences, my task is to narrow my focus to regard the most striking examples. Those I have selected are the Greek Phaëthon and Bellerophon and the Sumerian Etana. These three serve to illuminate key traits of the character of Lucifer as it is developed in the subsequent grimoire tradition, to be covered in *Praxis*. The notable absence from this company is Prometheus, who has become the tragic image of Lucifer, via Shelley as much as Aeschylus. For reasons that will become apparent, he is discussed in relation to the Enochian material in the later chapters, 'The Key' and 'A Mass of Blood and Feathers.'

The myth of Phaëthon's tragic course places the action on a cosmic scale. This evokes not only Isaiah, but its reflex in the apocalypse of Revelation, where it is not the fate of a single king, but a conflict that engulfs both heavens and earth. The resemblance of the story of Hêlêl Ben Šaḥar to that of Phaëthon has long been remarked. Gunkel[1] first made the identification; and Gruppe,[2] backed by the more recent work of Grelot,[3] advanced the thesis that Isaiah 14:12–15 preserved fragments of a lost West Semitic myth which corresponds to that of Phaëthon, recorded in Hesiod's *Theogony*,[4] Ovid's *Metamorphoses*, Nonnos' *Dionysiaca* and numerous other sources.

Phaëthon means 'the shining, glittering,' and, in a comparative analysis of Hesiod's text, can be identified as both the morning star and the son of Dawn (Êôs).

We remember how Phaëthon forces his father Helios to let him ride across the sky at the reins of his solar chariot, but loses control of the mighty team of horses, dropping the reins when confronted with the horrifying sight of Scorpio. The rising and plunging of the uncontrolled fiery chariot threatens to destroy the world. The ensuing disasters are very reminiscent of Revelation. The luckless youth is finally struck through with a thunderbolt hurled by Zeus, who thus restores the cosmic order. The boy pitches head first and aflame into the river Eridanus. The name of this river – variously identified with the earthly Po (called Eridanus by the Greeks), with the Rhine,[5] and the Rhône, (where the stench of his corpse is related in the *Argonautica*) – is significant. Eridanus was also located in the infernal Hades, which accords with the earlier version of the myth in which Hêlêl falls into Sheol, the netherworld; and the river is also identified as the celestial constellation of Eridanus itself. Of note is that the name Eridanus is derived from the Sumerian Eridu, the city sacred to Enki, god of water and cunning wisdom.[6]

These are what we would popularly accept as Luciferian motifs: challenge, pride, ascent, fire, fall; but I would rather caution that Ovid and Hesiod are an important part of our cultural heritage and that, given the paucity of scripture, have been drawn upon over a long period to colour the latter character of Lucifer. They seem familiar because they are now part of our common mythical substrata and make sense of unfamiliar allusions, such as the fall of the wormwood star in Revelation 8:10 and the unfolding planetary disaster so similar to that of Phaëthon. The corresponding section of Revelation bears citing:

> The first angel sounded, and there followed hail and fire mingled with blood, and they were cast upon the earth: and the third part of trees was burnt up, and all green grass was burnt up. And the second angel sounded, and as it were a great mountain burning with fire was cast into the sea: and the third part of the sea became blood; and the third part of the creatures which were in the sea, and had life, died; and the third part of the ships were destroyed. And the third angel sounded, and there fell a great star from heaven, burning as it were a lamp, and it fell upon the third part of the rivers, and upon the fountains of waters; and the name of the star is called Wormwood: and the third part of the waters became wormwood; and many men died of the waters, because they were made bitter. And the fourth angel sounded, and the third part of the sun was smitten, and the third part of the moon, and the third part of the stars; so as the third part of them was darkened, and the day shone not for a third part of it, and the night likewise.

It is tempting to identify Lucifer with cosmic catastrophe, the scorching of the Milky Way, the pole star shift, the heavy velvet of night with its scatter of stars ratcheting back, the meteor falling into boiling waters, the sun eclipsed and the moon running red. In doing so we could pursue the thesis of works such as *Hamlet's Mill*,[7] which build on Plato's reference to Phaëthon in *Timaeus*, and hang our tale upon this empyrean tapestry.

Important elements concur in the myths of Hêlēl and Phaëthon, not least their shared names and paternity, however, as Astour observes, 'no trace is left in the extant versions of the Phaëthon myth of the haughty design to seize the throne of heaven.'[8] A more striking affinity exists between Hêlēl and Bellerophon, whose disillusion with the gods and their injustice is attested in 30 tantalising fragments of Euripides' otherwise lost tragedy. Euripides puts these sacrilegious words in the mouth of Bellerophon:

> Does someone say there are indeed gods in heaven? There are not, if a man is willing not to rely foolishly on the antiquated reasoning.[9]

Tempting as it is, we must refrain from accepting the motive that Euripides attributes to Bellerophon for his theomachist action. Psychologising aside, the core structure of the myth can be given. Bellerophon flies to heaven on the back of the winged horse Pegasus, who is controlled by a golden bit of unsleeping metal clamped between its teeth. Driven ever higher by Bellerophon, catastrophe strikes. Pegasus is stung by a horse fly, the rider thrown from his mount. Bellerophon falls and is crippled for his rebellion against the gods.

A first, salient point of correspondence to observe here, in light of descriptions of Lucifer in the grimoires, is Bellerophon's youthful beauty.[10] It is another archaic Asiatic element preserved in the complex of myth[11] we have inherited: the beautiful, yet chaste, youth/hero who fatefully spurns the attentions of a goddess, frequently guised as a mortal woman.[12] The savage contrast between the desirable beauty of the rebellious hero and his eventual transformation, after the fall, into a crippled old man, limping, dressed in rags and condemned to wander, is resonant of the enigmatic and ambiguous relation of bright Lucifer to the old motley Devil.

A second observation, no less significant in view of certain themes that pertain to the role of Lucifer as first in the underworld, centres on the legend of Bellerophon's mastery of Pegasus. In brief, despite his ardent desire, he cannot tame the wild steed, born of the blood of the Gorgon. In the darkness of his sleep, Athena comes to him and gifts him the wondrous power that will enable him to tame Pegasus: the bit. It is only when we look beyond the English translation to delve in to the Greek texts that a distinct spectrum of meanings attached to the bit (Greek χαλινός, *chalinós*) becomes apparent. I commend the work of Marcel Detienne and Jean-Pierre Vernant[13] in this regard, and it is from their studies I draw the following. In Pindar's 13th *Olympian Ode*, certain charged terms describe the bit and its mode of action: *philtron* and *pharmakon* reveal its relationship to the magical elixirs, love philtres and binding poisons, whose use will always be associated with Circe and Medea. Placing the bit, which being metal is the unsleeping son of fire, in the same ambit as magically potent plants and their elixirs, is to draw an explicit connection between the chthonic realms of metallurgy and plant knowledge; and the cunning intelligence of Hephaestus and that of Athena, Medea et alia.

In a third and final observation, relating our resolute, theomachist hero to the mythology of Lucifer, I am indebted once more to Michael C. Astour and his analysis of a credible Semitic etymology for the name Bellerophon.[14] Unsatisfactorily explained even by the ancient Greeks, a Semitic derivation was first posited by H. Lewy. In a meticulous linguistic analysis, Astour traces the genealogy of the name to Baʿal-rāphôn, which translates as Baal (or lord) of healing.[15] The motif of healing is cogent, and belongs, as I previously noted, to the domain of underworld gods and the Rephaim. Baʿal-rāphôn corresponds in meaning to the Ugaritic Rpu-Bʿl, 'the healing lord,' the leader of the Rephaim, who was conceived and born in the underworld, and whose chief symbol was the serpent.[16]

The mythical beast Pegasus attests to the archaic oriental origin of the tale; the motif of the winged horse is certainly not Greek but can be traced to iconographic models of the Ancient Near East which combine the underworld and solar associations that we find intact in the Greek myths. According to Astour, 'the winged horse is, in a certain aspect, a mythico-iconographic synthesis of the destructive horse and of the eagle who carried Etana to heaven in order to get the "plant of birth."'[17]

Etana could be considered as the ur-myth of Lucifer, one which is concerned with the etiology and ideology of ancient kingship; and preserves the shamanic stratum out of which it arose. The origin of power is clear, in *Etana* I:[18]

(When) the sceptre of kingship came down from heaven,
[...] Ištar sought a king.

Etana is the earliest antediluvian king of Sumer,[19] whose existence
is recorded in the eponymous epic and corroborated by the Sumerian King List. He is, according to the epic, 'the king, the man who
ascended to heaven'; yet this is not a story of triumph. The poet who
composed the text expresses pessimism and laments:

> Where are they, the early kings, those of early days?
> They have not engendered, they are not reborn,
> Just as heaven is far away, my hand cannot reach them.
> In the broad earth, no man knows them...
> Having been given life by the gods,
> It was sought for Etana,
> But death is the share of mankind.

Clearly, stellar immortality has been apportioned to the early kings,
but eternal life on earth is not permitted. The Old Version of *Gilgameš* emphasises this:

> When the gods created mankind,
> Death for mankind they set aside,
> Life in their own hands retaining.

It is a prohibition that Genesis echoes: for man, immortality is to be
found in his children, his line, rather than his person. The destitu-
tion of childlessness is a recurring theme in texts from the ancient
world, and we should remember that the continuity of life, that is,
succession, as well as the art of healing, is of chthonic and stellar
provenance. By extension, the uprooting or extirpation of a line, is
an act of divine vengeance, or tyranny, as amply attested in the Bible.
   Etana's flight to heaven is accomplished with the aid of an eagle,
who is said to know the secret of the location of the plant of birth
(*šammu ša allâdi*), in the 'heights of heaven': the *ellâti*. He finds the

eagle after petitioning Šamaš, who had cast it into a pit and rendered it flightless as punishment for breaking the oath it swore with the serpent that they would not devour each other's young. The eagle with severed wings cast into the pit can be compared with Isaiah 14:15 where Hêlêl is brought down to Sheol (Hell), the lowest depths of the pit. The healing of the eagle by Etana can be read, on one level, as the restitution of divinely sanctioned kingship: the establishment of succession after the chaos of the flood.

The speech of the eagle offers up parallels with Hêlêl Ben Šaḥar of Isaiah; having planned evil in his heart, he proclaims, 'I will ascend and in the heavens I will dwell.'[20] This is startlingly similar to Isaiah 14:13, 'You have said in your heart I will ascend to the heavens, above the stars of El I will set my throne.'

The quest of Etana is also 'above the stars of El,' in the upper heaven of Ištar; but he loses his nerve when the eagle shows him how far above the earth they are, and the flight ends in a fall. The immediate consequence of the fall is unknown – the relevant passage is missing in all versions of the legend that have come down to us. Etana is, however, given the role of doorkeeper to the underworld, in a similar manner to Gilgameš who becomes an underworld deity.

At the risk of getting ahead of our story, I can remark that Lucifer in medieval demonology becomes the ruler in hell. Though we cannot make the direct correlation: Etana equals Hêlêl Ben Šaḥar, we are seeing the process of how the myths of kingship develop and this informs what was a previously closed text to us.

Yet perhaps here is where the trail is finally lost, as it enters into prehistory and the exploits of unknown shamans and their dizzying flights. Time is the great devourer. Again we are left with the redacted shamanic leitmotif, sans pinions and flight feathers, mewling in a dark pit for salvation. We too continue to grasp after Isaiah, hoping that it will suddenly break like the dark clouds and allow lances of sunlight to thrust through. Or perhaps we need to mantle ourselves like birds of prey and in doing so soar to comprehend on our widening gyre the entire span of the Near East before the flight can ever take us on towards Europe.

A King in Search of a Crown

Hêlēl Ben Šaḥar, the Lucifer of Isaiah, cannot be conveniently identified with a single mythological predecessor. Though it has been important to explore these myths, ultimately I side with Klaas Spronk
who, in his definitive study of the matter,[1] is damning. He concludes:

> [T]he idea of a god named Helel should be abandoned: Helel is no
> more than an epithet, which can be compared to the use of Akka-
> dian *ellu/elletu*, which can refer to, among other things, shining
> purity, to light, and also to gods, kings and priests.

It appears that there is not an 'Helel, son of Šaḥar' at all. In fact, the
use of *ben* does not necessarily even mean 'son,' but just as plausibly
'in relation to.' Šaḥar can be read, not only as a name, but as a term
connoting 'morning light, the dawn.' This leads back to the understanding that the figure under consideration is exactly what the
Greek translation of Heōsphóros has revealed, not Venus per se, but
the quality of its dawn-breaking light.

Any remnant myth in Isaiah 14 has been described by Prinsloo[2] as
'lacking a torso.' Hence, the difficulty of the task which this study
has set itself: our preferred certainty in this quest for origins is
unattainable. The Bible does not in this instance conceal a forbidden

figure, but tatters out into empty rags. For many looking for Lucifer, it will make profoundly disquieting reading. The hoped-for solitary figure has no single myth. His identity is legion. It is the first of many seeming abysses that we will encounter on our journey. We should stand a while and accept, even learn to savour, this cold rush of air.

Such a conclusion does not demythologise the text. When Isaiah evokes the idea of shining light it is no idle metaphor. The anointed king shines like a star because that is exactly what he is. Neither does the image refer solely to the Assyrian king. It is used in a wider sense, hinting at the opposition to El Elyon, literally god on high, from rival astral deities and the polytheism of a heavenly court or assembly. This position is expressed elsewhere in the Old Testament, as theological and social pressures force Judaism through the diffi-cult transition, from a sibling of Canaanite religion with a heavenly pantheon into a distinct divine dictatorship. Propagandist derision is directed at the stellar wisdom, and its consequent logic, the celes-tially ordained dominance of Babylon and Egypt. In Job 15:15 the changes are seen occuring, 'Behold, he putteth no trust in his saints; yea, the heavens are not clean in his sight.'[3] A sentiment echoed and reinforced in Job 25:5, 'Behold even to the moon, and it shineth not; yea, the stars are not pure in his sight.' The astral deities are steadily demoted to the status of clockwork angels and the storm god himself retreats to the outer darkness. Yet, this is to simplify a process of flux; the inability to entirely excise the idea of the starry court, or the concept of the divine king, proves to be an ongoing theological problem. The weight of scripture, the need to appeal to tradition for legitimacy, means that the door is left fatefully ajar. Satan slips through this chink, as a functionary of the heavenly tribunal, and drags with him the heavy ermine of Lucifer's stately robe, and as many companions as can be smuggled out under it.

The confusion Isaiah creates is in the appeal to a common trope in polytheism – that of the rival young god who attempts to overthrow the leader of the pantheon – but told from the perspective of the unassailable god of Israel. It assumes that the reader has all of these allusions at their disposal, drawn from the wider culture of the age, and can apply them with discretion. The text itself was designed to provide only the barest of outlines from which the holograph manifests in the mind's eye. Across the gulf of time, the image can still be summoned to flicker, but does so somewhat unsteadily at first. The flame of vision needs to be carefully cradled.

The intricacies of Isaiah should not be underplayed, because they set in motion the magic lantern that projects Lucifer onto the world stage. Returning to Prinsloo, his 'myth lacking a torso,' though highly quotable, could equally be expressed as a profusion of limbs in tumultuous motion, a definition which is more applicable in practice than the one that leaves the hero cold and anonymous on a mortuary slab.

Mark Shipp, in his exhaustive study of Isaiah 14, *Of Dead Kings and Dirges*,[4] insightfully concludes:

> While the passage does not relate specifically to a myth of the primordial fall of one of the members of the divine court, there are points of contact between the historical/mythological setting and its later theological appropriation by Church and Synagogue. If the 'King of Babylon' personified arrogance, presumption, and usurpation of the gods' prerogatives, how much more are these attributes characteristic of Satan, the great accuser of the Lord's elect and tyrannizer of creation?

The figure of Satan is aptly invoked. Witness Luke 10:18, (a direct linear descendant of Isaiah), 'And he said unto them, I beheld Satan as lightning fall from heaven.' A direct equivalence between Lucifer and Satan is made. Here Satan is struck down by the disciple's use of the name of Christ. The compulsion of malevolent spirits by the divine name(s) is no innovation, and can be traced back textually to the work of the Sumerian exorcists. Earlier in the same chapter (Luke 10:15) the ritual formula of being exalted to heaven and struck down to hell is given, 'And thou, Capernaum, which art exalted to heaven, shalt be thrust down to hell.' Evidently, Isaiah has been instrumental in the New Testament, and thence the burgeoning demonology of Christianity that has informed the structure of

European magic. By returning through the door that Satan slipped through, demonology is reclaimed as chthonic: the roots of religion, rather than an inverse hierarchy with ritual actions as mere reactive blasphemy.

The increasing academic consensus is that despite the mythic elements of Isaiah 14, exegesis should not, primarily, be focused on the search for a mythological figure. When the lines are read in context they are found to be a dirge. This is indicated by the known formula, *Oh N.N., how fallen art thou*, an equivalent to the current British, *The King is dead, long live the King*. In Isaiah the formula is employed as a *mashal* to attack kingship which has overstepped its bounds. Isaiah is mocking and provocative, not mourning the death of the king, but, on the contrary, gloating. The opening – *Oh Lucifer, how fallen art thou* – parodies a stylised form: the lament for the king. It then deviates to become not a pæan, but a crow song over his corrupting corpse.

What is read, in hindsight, as an attack on an entity, Lucifer, is erroneous. It is the concept of apotheosis, the deification of the king after his death, that is the original target: the elevation of a king to the company of heaven being considered by the prophet as overstepping the bounds of that institution. Context is critical, and this is given in Isaiah 14:9–12, the preceding lines:

> Hell from beneath is moved for thee to meet thee at thy coming: it stirreth up the dead for thee, even all the chief ones of the earth; it hath raised up from their thrones all the kings of the nations. All they shall speak and say unto thee, Art thou also become weak as we? art thou become like unto us? Thy pomp is brought down to the grave, and the noise of thy viols: the worm is spread under thee, and the worms cover thee.

The king, cast down into Sheol, meets the Rephaim, the mighty dead; he has become as one with them. Here the dead begin to speak, but not as one would expect; they are rendered impotent by the parodist, an important stage in the sequence of reversals of fortune and position.

Only warily can biblical tradition be used to reconstruct a picture of the Rephaim. These texts are far removed from the living tradition of the mighty dead as encountered in the Ugaritic texts.[5] Biblical writers (the Deuteronomists in particular) are more concerned with restricting the rituals to the dead within Israelite society, than with providing an accurate portrayal of their rivals.

The term 'rephaim' can variously refer to the ancient ancestral dead; fallen warriors; and the Neolithic inhabitants of Canaan. Earlier writers, dependent on the biblical sources, suggested the Rephaim as minor deities or cultic functionaries; a tribal group; or chariot warriors. All these definitions have been argued over ad nauseum, and perhaps the most clear position to take is that they are the spirits of the deified ancestral dead who annually return to the upper world to feast.

Our understanding of the Rephaim has deepened on account of the Ugaritic texts; and the consensus that the meaning of the West Semitic root *rp* is to heal. This is the same root encountered in the more familiar guise of the archangel Raphael. Healing is a power of the dead, and most commonly represented by the serpent. As the dead exist in the hinterland between gods and humans, they have the strength to intercede against the demons of disease. In Catholicism this tradition continues in the cult of the saints. The ancestral dead, and the gods themselves, can be the source of illness: the result of lapses in ritual protocol, or from accidental slight. It is the role of the ritual specialist to divine what has occurred and prescribe a remedy to restore the balance of relationships whose disruption has created disease.

An example of such a healing oracle can be found in KTU 2.124, wherein a prescription is given from beyond the grave for a sick child.[6] The function of the Rephaim here is comparable to the Mesopotamian Anunnaki. We should be mindful when approaching this source that, as Pitard observes:[7]

> In the entire collection of narrative poetic texts from Ugarit few are as obscure and difficult to interpret as the rpum fragments.

Rarely have the ambiguities of a vowelless script and the piece-meal preservation of so many damaged lines conspired so power-fully to frustrate attempts at drawing decisive conclusions about a text.

I have noted this, and thus do not venture into speculation where even specialist scholars fear to tread: my focus is on how notions of the Rephaim in the Ugaritic texts dovetail with the references to them in Old Testament sources. The depiction of the Rephaim has already passed through the matrix of Canaanite religion before being used in the Bible for political ends. The Ugaritic texts are therefore used to support my argument, and to fill in the omissions in the biblical account, but with these caveats.

In the Ugaritic texts, a distinguished group of *rp'um* in the nether-world are the divinised shades of the dead. The 'shades' of the dead evokes the image of shadows, but there is a more salient implication: that of protection, as in Isaiah 30:2-3 and Ezekiel 31, where the king is likened to a mighty tree. This throws the image into three dimen-sions. Attempts to characterise the Rephaim as the 'weakened dead' uses 'shade' in only its most cursory sense. Such usage is, alas, still currency in some academic texts – particularly those underpinned by a religious bias, whether conscious or otherwise. When Hilde-gard of Bingen wrote of how the devil 'overshadows [the soul] and obscures it with shadows and the smoke of his blackness,' she com-bined smouldering Gehenna and the Greek Hades with the specific idea of the shade as malefic, and in contradistinction to the living light of Christ. This is a critical cultural misunderstanding; the cool shade sought as respite in the East becomes the flight from the light in the dark of northern Europe. I cannot give a complete history of shadows, and will limit myself to the example of Lucifer becoming Lucifuge as arguably descending from the legacy of Isaiah, by way of Psellus's classification in *On the Work of Demons*, that was carried into *Le Grand Grimoire* and *Le Dragon Rouge*.

Rp'um is a special title, reserved for kings, heroes, warriors and rulers; among them are the *rp'im qdmyn*, the primeval dead, the spirits of ancient ancestors who, in the Ugaritic texts, are cared for and invoked for protection in order to give health and strength.[8] How are the dead kings and Rephaim summoned? Quite simply, by the pronouncement of their names and the offering of sacrifice which they are then invited to partake in. The recollection and recitation of the names of the dead ensures their continued existence. This provides the answer to the initiatic riddle, *what is it that does not corrupt in the grave?* Though I have not found academic corroboration for the idea, I would suggest that not directly naming Sargon II is, as well as for the reasons previously explored, part of the process of his erasure, and a deliberate component in the curse formula of Isaiah.

The dead can also be forcibly summoned out of season, as the witch of Endor does. They are then conjured and bound in the same way as the standard operating procedure of European demonology, as found in the grimoires.[9]

These mighty ones are the entourage of the Sun (personified as the Ugaritic goddess Šapšu), as it travels through the netherworld. In the KTU 1.20–22, this host comes travelling for three nights from the netherworld, with horses and chariots, to attend a communion ritual on behalf of the new king.[10] According to Spronk, this marks the New Year at the Spring equinox, which celebrates the return of Baal to life. The power that Baal has, of overcoming death, is transferred to the king in this ritual. Dietrich and Loretz[11] have shown that Baal, as leader of the Rephaim, is titled *rpu-b'l* in the Ugaritic texts. He provides healing and this allows us to deduce a lineage for him, as all West Semitic healer gods descend from the Sumerian Ninazu and his son Ningišzida, whose symbol is the familiar caduceus which is popularly and erroneously considered as Greek. The healer god is the 'god of the stick,' and the god as stick.[12] The magician is then considered as the one who dominates and wields the power of the stick, whether in the form of the wand, or thyrsus, or stang, or sceptre.

The Rephaim arrive at night, at the threshing floors and plantations, the typical abode of ghosts. It was the place that marked the intersection of mourning rites with fertility as the gift of the dead.[13] In this liminal place the Rephaim are given offerings of apples and ambrosia as well as olives and gourds, fattened by the rain brought by Baal. As in all cultures, other than our terminal own, the dead must be properly feasted; this is also a key principle in working with the spirits of place, whether faery, ancestor or animal. The threshing floor as place of ghosts cannot but remind me of our own harvest rituals, and the confession of Isobel Gowdie who flew like a straw in the wind at the behest of the Devil.

The Rephaim are fallen warriors, but have another guise, that of birds – which recalls the feathered dead of the Sumerian nether-world, whom Enkidu's chilling dream relates in the *Epic of Gilgameš*:

> They are clothed like birds with wings for covering, they see no light, they sit in darkness. I entered the house of dust and I saw the kings of the earth, their crowns put away for ever; rulers and princes, all those who once wore kingly crowns and ruled the world in the days of old.

Our culture habitually associates winged, otherworldly beings with angels, yet the iconography is undoubtedly part of an archaic, pan-cultural heritage where they were the feathered dead of the chthonic realm. The underworld has not been democratised in *Gilgameš* or the cultures of Ugarit or Canaan: the dead with status and power are those who achieved renown in life. KTU 1.21 implores them with the spare ritual formula, 'May the Rephaim flutter to the holy place, may the ghosts flutter to the holy place.' A mockery of this entire ritual complex can be found in Ezekiel 39:17–30, in which the birds, at the command of Yahweh, feast on the slaughtered dead of the enemies of Israel:

> And, thou son of man, thus saith the Lord God; Speak unto every feathered fowl, and to every beast of the field, Assemble your-selves, and come; gather yourselves on every side to my sacrifice that I do sacrifice for you, even a great sacrifice upon the moun-tains of Israel, that ye may eat flesh, and drink blood. Ye shall eat the flesh of the mighty, and drink the blood of the princes of the

earth, of rams, of lambs, and of goats, of bullocks, all of them fatlings of Bashan. And ye shall eat fat till ye be full, and drink blood till ye be drunken, of my sacrifice which I have sacrificed for you. Thus ye shall be filled at my table with horses and chariots, with mighty men, and with all men of war, saith the Lord God.

The necrotic revenge banquet is repeated in Revelation 19:17–21, where the same fate befalls the beast and the false prophet:

And I saw an angel standing in the sun; and he cried with a loud voice, saying to all the fowls that fly in the midst of heaven, Come and gather yourselves together unto the supper of the great God; That ye may eat the flesh of kings, and the flesh of captains, and the flesh of mighty men, and the flesh of horses, and of them that sit on them, and the flesh of all men, both free and bond, both small and great. And I saw the beast, and the kings of the earth, and their armies, gathered together to make war against him that sat on the horse, and against his army. And the beast was taken, and with him the false prophet that wrought miracles before him, with which he deceived them that had received the mark of the beast, and them that worshipped his image. These both were cast alive into a lake of fire burning with brimstone. And the remnant were slain with the sword of him that sat upon the horse, which sword proceeded out of his mouth: and all the fowls were filled with their flesh.

The horrific ekphrasis of the apocalyptic vision only makes sense when related to its original context, as a parodic inversion of the feast of the Rephaim. Rather than being transfixed by this grotesque vista, instead recall that the return of the dead is linked to the seasonal Spring migration. The voices of the dead are not *equated with* birdsong, but *as* birdsong; the many-tongued fire of choral dawn which greets those who have made it through the arduous night journey. Notable too are the many bird forms found in the spirit heraldry of the *Lemegeton,* as descendants of this tradition.

The Rephaim intercede in times of crisis and even join battles; the parallels between this and the European tradition of the Wild Hunt are striking. I am not suggesting a direct genealogy, rather, that they belong to the same underlying mythic realm that acknowledges the chthonic and astral survival of the mighty dead. The difference, as we head north into Europe, is the shift in focus to the Winter fire festivals as the season of the dead, rather than the green fuse of Spring and Easter still fervently celebrated in the Orthodox East, Islamic New Year and so forth.[14]

Returning to Isaiah, the text describes not the enduring supernatural strength of the Rephaim, but their ineffectual weakness. Perhaps Isaiah is deliberately invoking the root *rph*, meaning weakness, rather than *rp*, to heal. This is, indeed, the choice made in the Rabbinical exegesis of *b.Ket* 111b and *Bereshit Rabbah* 26, 7, in which the entire concept of the divine nature of the king and the hero is mocked. The king of Babylon is cursed, not to rise to his stellar destiny as 'shining' (*hêlēl*), but to be cast out of his grave. This is profoundly shocking, and sacrilegous to the culture upon which Isaiah pronounces his curse. It is not without precedent: a similar fate is meted out to the Pharoah in Ezekiel 32, which is clearly reminiscent of the combat myth of Marduk and Tiamat.[15] Isaiah attacks pride: the king must be humbled into remembrance that he will die, and not mistake his rule under the auspices of divine power as his own divinity. He is not attacking Hêlēl alone, his threat hangs over any potential ruler of Israel, whether gentile usurper or Jew. As with most propaganda, the intended target is not an external enemy, but the vassals of the state.

It can be convincingly argued that Canaanite conceptions of stellar ascension were modified by Egyptian ideas. The Pyramid texts proclaim, 'You ascend to the sky as a star, as the morning star.' The king is described as 'the one who does not go down,' i.e. to the netherworld. He is variously identified with the never-setting circumpolar stars; the morning star, because it leaves the world of the dead before the sun rises; and Sirius, whose appearance marked the life-giving inundation of the Nile. In the early period, the dead king was identified with Osiris as the ruler of the dead. Later this was fused with the concept of stellar ascension, and in this respect with the constellation of Orion.

The influence of Egyptian cult on the Bible is undeniable; in Genesis 50:2–3, for example, Israel (Jacob) evidently undergoes hybrid funeral rites:

> And Joseph commanded his servants the physicians to embalm his father: and the physicians embalmed Israel. And forty days were fulfilled for him; for so are fulfilled the days of those which are embalmed: and the Egyptians mourned for him threescore and ten days.

Note the use of the Venus number – 40 – her retrograde station,[16] and the Egyptian decan number – 70 – the number of days Sirius is absent beneath the horizon.

Further parallels can be found in surviving Ugaritic and Phoenician texts. The king would go to his death in the West with the setting sun and, after a period in the underworld, would rise renewed as the morning star and join the company of the gods in eternal life. Critically, we should note that the living king is identified with the Sun, and, in his post mortem state, he is identified with a star. Analogous is the composite identification of Lucifer with the Sun, the planet Venus as morning star, the fixed star Sirius and the constellation Orion: an alloy compounded in the same fiery infernal forge as the deified kings of the ancient Near East.

Egyptian religion is tangential to my intention in this thesis; of interest is how these Canaanite borrowings were absorbed into Israel's Yahweh cult as he underwent the transformation from tribal god to overarching deity. My argument is that it is this process of astral deification to which Lucifer is the legitimate heir.

Isaiah claims that the king of Babylon seeks more than stellar immortality, he hunts a pre-eminent position in the heavens: he desires, not merely to join the company of El, but to ascend to the throne of the most high on his holy mountain, Zaphon. His hubris demands punishment. The text goes on to attack the entire stellar hierarchy[17] in Isaiah 24:21–23:

> And it shall come to pass in that day, that the Lord shall punish the host of the high ones that are on high, and the kings of the earth upon the earth. And they shall be gathered together, as prisoners are gathered in the pit, and shall be shut up in the prison, and after many days shall they be visited. Then the moon shall be confounded, and the sun ashamed, when the Lord of hosts shall reign in mount Zion, and in Jerusalem, and before his ancients gloriously.

By placing kingship centre stage, Isaiah's polemic finally yields to us. The deified dead, venerated as a heavenly host of warrior stars are the company to whom the king of Babylon, the shining one, aspires. Isaiah overturns the expected narrative: the body of the king is denied a grave and the proper burial rites. He is thus denied ascension to the stars and denied cult.

The entire concept of a rival divine authority is anathema to Yahweh, in his transformation into the monotheistic tyrant of the post-exilic period. In Isaiah 13:10 Yahweh even darkens the sky to prevent the sun, moon and stars being seen. The king of Babylon is a demonised representative of the intolerable threat to the exclusive dominance of this ambitious tribal god, and embodies an earlier stellar tradition – and beneath that a chthonic one – which must be erased, and with it, the memory of a company of gods and the cults to the royal dead. It is, in fact, Yahweh who is guilty of seeking to set himself above all others.

Isaiah is a composite text, written by many hands and spanning a period of religious and political turmoil. It is both pre- and post-exilic: its composition stretches from the period when Israel was a vassal state of Assyria to the fall of the Assyrian king, Sargon II. It is synchronous with the subsequent rise of Babylon, the exile with the destruction of the Temple in 587 BCE and the return of the diaspora in 538 BCE – the foundations of the Second Temple being subsequently laid in 520 BCE. Isaiah is, therefore, a political instrument in the changing conceptions of divinity and the role of the king. The demonisation of Lucifer should be read in relation to this process. Whereas the retribution in Isaiah is enacted as a result of the king overstepping the bounds of kingship, the attack on the institution itself issues from another quarter, and one with a far more radical agenda, which forever marks the destiny of the fallen one.

The Invisible God

Deuteronomy is delivered in the form of the purported sermons of
Moses. Though ostensibly a book of law, at heart it is an attempt
to explain away the consistent and crushing failures of Yahweh. It
is marked by the genesis of its composition, namely the trauma of
the Babylonian exile, with the text itself brought together from the
seventh to the fifth centuries BCE. As a result of its extended composition, the text contains evidence of monolatrous and monotheistic
theologies.

Displacement, discord and disaster often precipitate apocalyptic
thinking, and that is precisely the case here. Deuteronomy appeals
to the state origin myth of Moses and the promise of a land to be
ruled by their god, recounting the bloody conquest of the already
occupied territory of Canaan. Here is a god who brooks no rivals.[1]
This rousing account of entitlement and slaughter, of inflexible law
and order, would have been sustenance for the exiles who returned,
radicalised, to build the state of Israel.

Deuteronomy is only one part of the project of the Deuteronomists, who hammered Joshua, Judges, Samuel and Kings into a
more or less unified history of Israel and also influenced elements of
Jeremiah. The combined texts were designed to provide the only possible explanation for failure, that it was not Yahweh who had broken

his covenant, but the people who had not submitted to the justice of his yoke; it is identical logic to that of Isaiah. Though the fate of the pagans may appal, the community is also tyrannised by the law, with women and rebellious children summarily stoned to death for their infractions. The internal enemy, the heretic, is always the most reviled, and required, element in the conclave of the pure.

The Deuteronomists have become the lens for all subsequent readings of Isaiah, and thus their theological position needs to be clearly stated: first, a belief in one God who is heard but not seen; second, an emphasis on Moses, Exodus and the covenant at Sinai; and third, a secular view of kingship and no theogony, with hostility to many temple traditions, practices, and a rejection of the concept of atonement. I will examine these points in turn to expose the underlying unity of the Deuteronomists' agenda.

Firstly, the insistence on a god who is seen and not heard draws down anger upon those who create graven images and unleashes genocide against those who worship idols. This idea also tramples on the testament of Isaiah, who actually saw God. Instead, the Deuteronomists exalt Moses, who only heard God.[2] The denial of seeing God is continued in the New Testament with John 1:18 declaring, 'No man hath seen God at any time; the only begotten Son, which is in the bosom of the Father, he hath declared him.'[3]

In Deuteronomy 4:19 it is stated that God has no countenance, and that the celestial company should also be shunned, a theme that is now becoming familiar:

And lest thou lift up thine eyes unto heaven, and when thou seest the sun, and the moon, and the stars, even all the host of heaven, shouldest be driven to worship them, and serve them, which the Lord thy God hath divided unto all nations under the whole heaven.

This attack fuses Babylonian ideas with Canaanite ones, seeking to forever remove the celestial deities and set up Yahweh as lone ruler, rather than part of a company of heaven.[4]

This was a major plank of the Deuteronomic Reform, and it is an attack on the original myth and pattern of rulership which is recast as the reason for the fall of Jerusalem. The history of divine kingship within Israel they sought to completely condemn, and where possible, elide. However, a glimpse of the previous state organisation can be seen in Lamentations 4:14-15, in which the host of heaven is rejected for failing to save the city:

> They have wandered as blind men in the streets, they have polluted themselves with blood, so that men could not touch their garments. They cried unto them, Depart ye; it is unclean; depart, depart, touch not: when they fled away and wandered, they said among the heathen, They shall no more sojourn there.

This passage preserves evidence that, although the celestial deities may have originally been Canaanite or Mesopotamian, they seem to have been an intrinsic element of the Jerusalem cult rather than a foreign imposition.

Secondly, the Deuteronomists emphasise Mosaic law. It is regarded as the final word: it is the Will of God entire. This is the same damning finality that we find in Islam with its decree that Mohammed is 'the seal on the prophets'; or, in capitalist theology, with Francis Fukuyama's now derided 'end of history.' Such fanatical pronouncements are always doomed, as time is a river which cannot be dammed. Deuteronomy is, in essence, a binding ritual: one which ties Israel to Yahweh as a vassal is bound to their Lord. Ironically, this relationship is based on the Assyrian model of kingship and vassal states, though Deuteronomy is fervently opposed to any kingship that does not serve Yahweh and his unyielding Law. The covenant is succinctly expressed in Deuteronomy 6:4, 'Hear, O Israel: The Lord our God is one Lord.'

The fate of the nation is predicated on absolute loyalty to the tribal god. By extension, any failure or suffering wrought on the nation is not attributable to the weakness of Yahweh, but is the result of the inconstancy of his people. The inevitable consequence of this thinking is an internal witch hunt. A search through scripture for the ideological origins of the witch panic of the early modern period would not begin and end with Revelation, but would have to encompass Deuteronomy as one of its most important precursors. The covenant, which still remains the vital element in Judaism, is later interpreted in Christianity as replaced by faith in Christ; though this new covenant carries with it the same terrible consequences. It brooks no rivals, and when they are absent, turns in on itself to create and extirpate them.

The worship of 'foreign' gods and goddesses carries the sentence of death in the purifying flames. The planting of groves is forbidden, as is the setting up of *ašerah*, the sacred tree or pole. Deuteronomy 12:2–3 is unsparing in its pogrom:

> Ye shall utterly destroy all the places, wherein the nations which ye shall possess served their gods, upon the high mountains, and upon the hills, and under every green tree. And ye shall overthrow their altars, and break their pillars, and burn their groves with fire; and ye shall hew down the graven images of their gods, and destroy the names of them out of that place.

This holocaust requires the destruction of all evidence that the Israelite's religion belongs to the shared cultural heritage and religious koiné of the region. The previous position of biblical scholarship was expressed by Kaufmann, in *The Religion of Israel,* who boldly stated, 'Israelite religion was an original creation of the people of Israel. It was absolutely different from anything the pagan world ever knew.'[5] This has been utterly disproved, and now the consensus acknowledges that Yahweh absorbed many of the attributes, deeds and epithets of the Canaanite El. In *The Storm God in the Ancient Near East,* Alberto Green concludes, 'The evident similarities between the Canaanite and Hebrew mythological texts and agricultural ritual confirm that in the earlier stages, Canaanite and Israelite religion were practically identical.'[6]

This should be sufficient warning to those who seek to damn the Bible in its entirety and, in doing so, miss the fact that it preserves a deep stratum of pagan and even shamanic elements. It should also warn against reading works, such as Kaufmann's, without assuming an inherent religious and political bias in the presentation of the material.

The covenant of Moses emphatically pronounced in Deuteronomy is different to that of Isaiah. The covenant, for Isaiah, is restored by atonement: the healing accomplished by the king, who is the son of god and enthroned in the sanctuary of the Temple. This leads us neatly on to the third position of the Deuteronomists: that kingship is placed beneath Yahweh. This is the coup itself, outlined in Deuteronomy 17:14–20. Whilst Isaiah attacked the king of Babylon, it is the entire concept of divine kingship that the Deuteronomists have in their sights. Their king is to be controlled by the priesthood. Along with this, many elements of temple practice are to be swept aside, from which they, as Levites, have been excluded. It was a definitive attack on the form of monarchy exemplified by Solomon and the royal cult of Jerusalem. When Deuteronomy 17:17 pronounces 'neither shall he multiply wives to himself, that his heart turn not away,' it can only have Solomon in mind. Isaiah was within this Temple tradition, but it is easy to see how his attack on the king of Babylon could be read to suit the Deuteronomist agenda. The conflict between the Deuteronomists' vision and the royal cult is only one in a series of internecine struggles that erupt in all religions as different factions, priesthoods, administrators, oligarchs and monarchs vie for dominance. A fight that continued between monarch and papacy, church and state, in Europe with often devastating consequences.

To understand the Deuteronomists position requires knowing how the Temple functioned. The Temple existed since Solomon and was the house of the Lord, built by Hiram of Tyre. As I have already remarked, it was the King of Tyre who suffered the same fate as Lucifer; and this is no accident. The Temple was modelled on the conception of the structure of the divinely ordered universe.

The interior was divided by an elaborate woven veil which separated the Holy of Holies from 'the garden of Eden.' Behind the veil was the chariot throne with its cherubim, as described in 1 Chronicles 28 and 2 Chronicles 3. Naturally, these idols were anathema to the Deuteronomists. More shockingly still, the throne was not empty but was sat upon by the king himself, who ruled as the Lord. We see the divine monarch described in 1 Chronicles 29:23, 'Then Solomon sat on the throne of the Lord as king instead of David his father, and prospered; and all Israel obeyed him.' The verse enables us to elucidate Ezekiel's famous vision of God as a fiery man on a throne before whom he prostrates himself. It is a remembrance of kingship and, what is more, a common model of kingship that was found throughout the Near East.

The king is a son of the Lord and born from the womb of the morning. He is the son of the Sun goddess, a tradition echoed by the woman clothed with the Sun in Revelation 12. He is raised up and anointed, given dominance over the chaotic powers of river and sea, takes the throne, speaks the word of the Lord and upholds His divine law. These elements can all be found in Psalms, and draw heavily on Canaanite myths of El and Baal.

The Canaanite derived model of kingship replaced the previous power structure of Yahwism, that had endured until the time of Samuel, in which there was no king but Yahweh and the role of the prophet and judges was pre-eminent.[7] The Deuteronomists sought a return to an order closer to these 'original values,' and a similar form of theocratic organisation; but with the king as a captive tool of the priesthood. In their favour we can note their emphatic concern for the poor; although their apparent social justice is concurrent with a centralisation of power, and in Deuteronomy 27–30, cursing into conformity those who transgress the strict rules of the community.

The final, critical component of the kingly function is the ritual of atonement. In the Second Temple period this was performed by the high priest, but previously priest and king were a unified role. The king would perform sacrifice to atone for the sins of the people, taking on the burden of sin, sprinkling blood upon the altar and making burned offerings. This was an annual communal rite. Two identical goats were selected and their fate decided by lot, as described in Leviticus 16:[8]

> And he shall take the two goats, and present them before the Lord at the door of the tabernacle of the congregation. And Aaron shall cast lots upon the two goats; one lot for the Lord, and the other lot for the scapegoat. And Aaron shall bring the goat upon which the Lord's lot fell, and offer him for a sin offering. But the goat, on which the lot fell to be the scapegoat, shall be presented alive before the Lord, to make an atonement with him, and to let him go for a scapegoat into the wilderness.

One goat is sacrificed in the Temple, the other is given to the wilderness. I will lay out the full detail of the ritual, as it has profound implications for *Praxis*.

The priest places both his hands on the scapegoat and a woollen scarlet thread is fastened about its head. As is said in Isaiah 1:18, 'Come now, and let us reason together, saith the Lord: though your sins be as scarlet, they shall be as white as snow; though they be red like crimson, they shall be as wool.'

In ritual terms, this pronouncement is the confession, a requisite preliminary in the sequence of magical acts that allows for purification and the entering into the divine presence. The goat was led past ten stations, at each of which it refused food and drink. Once it reached the mountain top, the red thread was divided, one half tied about a stone and the goat ceremoniously thrown to its death. The passage cited in Isaiah alludes to the miraculous changing of the colour of the wool from red to white, a prodigy (or less charitably, a sleight of hand) which ceased forty years before the destruction of the Second Temple.[9]

There is evidence that the king was once identified with the sin offering of blood, but that a substitution was made. In the Babylonian New Year ritual the same kind of switch occurs: a goat is given to Ereškigal in lieu of a human sacrifice. The *as-if* formula – based on analogical, rather than later symbolic, thinking – is the originary principle in all magic, as indeed all human culture. In urban folklore, the Satanic sacrifice of a goat glyphs that of a human, though evidence of such practice has never been provided. Even Crowley's quip about human sacrifice, that is still cited by Evangelicals, is an as-if that refers, not to murder, but to masturbation.[10]

Christ serves the sacrificial role as *piaculum* in the expiatory rite of crucifixion in the New Testament, with much reference to his blood. His is the 'new covenant' which eclipses that of Moses. The crucifixion can, in this sense, be seen as equivalent to the atonement ritual. Christ is cast as the scapegoat, who, like Lucifer, descends to hell (the harrowing) and then ascends to sit at the side of his father (stellar apotheosis). Tertullian developed a variant of this idea, in which both the goat offered at the Temple and the one in the wilderness represented Christ. From the ritual of atonement leap forth a series of blood taboos that are expressed in Leviticus 17:

> And whatsoever man there be of the house of Israel, or of the strangers that sojourn among you, that eateth any manner of blood; I will even set my face against that soul that eateth blood, and will cut him off from among his people. For the life of the flesh is in the blood: and I have given it to you upon the altar to make an atonement for your souls: for it is the blood that maketh an atonement for the soul. Therefore I said unto the children of Israel, No soul of you shall eat blood, neither shall any stranger that sojourneth among you eat blood.

There are vestiges here of shamanic hunting taboos, and perhaps we can even glimpse further into prehistory and the 'not eating of your own kill' prohibitions discussed by Chris Knight in *Blood Relations*, that form the menstrual backdrop to my own *Apocalyptic Witchcraft*. Blood is a sacred, potent and dangerous substance. The violation of the blood taboo will be discussed further when I turn to Genesis and Enoch. For now, the element of the ritual that concerns us is the fate of the sin offering, the goat for Azazel, in a rite that the Deuteronomists categorically rejected. The disputed identity of Azazel, and his role in the mythos of Lucifer, is the focus of the next chapter.

To conclude, there is good reason to pause and reflect on the sabbatic implications of this complex of symbols. The kingship model that the Deuteronomists spurn has a shamanic origin. The divine son is the result of the *hieros gamos* in the underworld, between the king as ruler of the dead and the goddess who is the gate of birth and death. A descent and ultimate ascent to the stars is a story of flight, the primary signifier of the shaman's power, the earlier figure who stands behind the king: motifs that can be found in the *Epic of Gilgameš* and the *Legend of Etana*. I have argued, in my previous work, that the witches' sabbat serves the same purpose and preserves this mythic arrangement.

A Goat for Azazel

In the rite of atonement a sinful goat stands as the symbol of rebellion:
it ascends on high and is cast down to inglorious death. It differs
from the Temple offering, in which the goat is burned; in Hebrew
the word for this kind of sacrifice, עֹלָה (alah), means 'ascent,' whereas
the goat for Azazel is clearly *fallen*. It was perhaps inevitable that
this motif would be read in tandem with the fall of Hêlēl in Isaiah.
It is essential to survey the scene from this high ground, to take in
not only the points of contact, but the errors that have crept in as
a result of this identification: in particular the supposed demonic
identity of Azazel.

The initial problem is the meaning of the word Azazel, עֲזָאזֵל in
Hebrew. Three possibilities have been proposed: the first that it
refers to a place; the second, that it means scapegoat (literally 'the
goat that goes'); and third, that Azazel is the name of a demon. I
will deal with each in turn. The explanation that Azazel refers to a
'rugged place,' the cliff from which the goat is thrown, is insecure on
etymological grounds, and most likely represents a rationalisation.
This is the Rabbinic position, which accounts for its persistence, but
it must be considered a false etiology. The combination of 'goat' and
'go away' is the easy route, taken by the Septuagint, Vulgate and KJV,
sidestepping the issue of Azazel as a proper name and that trouble-

some preposition: *for*. The third, and most problematic, option to explore is the existence of Azazel as a demonic entity of the wilderness.

Leviticus 16:8 prescribes 'One lot for the Lord and the other lot for Azazel.' The implication of the line is that Azazel – as a proper noun – refers to a being who has some kind of equivalence to Yahweh. Both, after all, receive an identical sacrifice. Understandably, this has been seized upon both by those looking for an alternative pantheon to oppose Christianity, and by demonologists combing through the Bible for names of the enemy. Furthermore, it represents a developed scholarly position, which argues that Azazel was an early Semitic god of the flocks. This position relies upon connecting the goat with the שְׂעִירִים (*seirim*, the 'hairy ones'), of Isaiah 13:21, 34:14, Leviticus 17:7 and 2 Chronicles 11:15. In the KJV, *seirim* is markedly translated as 'satyrs' in the same passage that *lilith* is given as 'screech owl.' These hairy ones are also the 'roes and hinds of the field' which the Shulamite invokes in the Song of Songs. This contextual argument is seductive, though not entirely straightforward. When we read on in Leviticus, sacrificing to *seirim* is specifically forbidden, in 17:7: And they shall no more offer their sacrifices unto devils, after whom they have gone a whoring. This shall be a statute for ever unto them throughout their generations.

Here the KJV gives 'devils' as the translation of *seirim*. It would be incongruous to sanction, on the one hand, a goat *for* Azazel, as supposed leader of the *seirim*, and in the following verses to outlaw such a sacrifice. The conclusion must be that the authors of Leviticus did not consider Azazel to be a devil. Though the Bible is wrought with contradictions – due often to competing conceptions and different strata of overlapping, edited texts – this is not the case with Leviticus. The contradiction of Azazel as devil, alongside the prohibition of sacrifice to *seirim*, is a logical impossibility.

The objection to this proposal is that the goat for Azazel cannot be counted as a sacrifice or offering as it is 'unclean,' burdened as it is with the sin of the people. I would suggest that this is an elegant piece of sophistry, aimed at cleaving the identities of Azazel and Yahweh who, as must be continually stressed, share an identical offering and are treated in equivalent terms in the text. It would seem highly unlikely that identical offerings would be made to utterly distinct divinities.

Scholars confidently predicted that further evidence of Azazel as a major devil would be forthcoming, a reasonable assumption that would make sense of the methodology of comparative mythology. However, an ivory plaque from Megiddo, which was hailed as proof of a goatish Azazel demon, is now very much in doubt. The absence of archaeological data leaves four mentions of Azazel in the Bible, all of which occur in Leviticus; this does not suggest a demon of any status, let alone the demonised god of another tribe. Without further corroboration, the demonic thesis must be cast into doubt. It is a problem that cannot be sensibly ignored, though I will note that this remains the position of the majority of scholars in this field.

In a reaction against the dominant demonological position of scholarship, some academics now seek to radically excise the demonic from the Old Testament. A prominent example of this standpoint is Judit M. Blair's *De-demonising the Old Testament*.[1] Such an approach understands the hostility of the Deuteronomists to the rite of atonement specifically in terms of their opposition to the role of kingship in the rite. It therefore requires no demonic component. Whilst convenient, I find this to be ideologically driven, another attempt to return to the argument of the uniqueness of Israelite religion in the face of overwhelming evidence to the contrary. Again, this highlights the difficulty of biblical scholarship; it remains in the grip of people with very specific religious interests which they wish not only to defend, but to advance.

Facing this impasse, it is apposite to turn again to the etymology, which is, after all, archaeology of another sort. Azazel is a homophone for Asael: 'Strong God.' Such is the rendering we find in the Midrash, Qumran scrolls and the Enochic literature. Hayim Tawil,[2] in 'Azazel The Prince of the Steepe,' argues that Azazel is a 'scribal metathesis,' that is, a rearrangement of the letters, and means, in fact, 'fierce god.' He goes on to identify him as the Canaanite Mot, god of the netherworld; an identification that has not gained acceptance in the academy. Likewise, attempts to find the identity of this figure in any other pantheon have met the same stony fate. Yet perhaps Tawil has the half of it. The figure of Yahweh in the Old Testament is frankly unpleasant, capricious and violent. He is such an ugly figure that the later Gnostics would consider him the demiurge. Here was a god who needed propitiating and who smote his own, a typical storm god in the mould of El and Baal. There was none of the asymmetric dualism that flowers in Revelation, no opposer at this early stage of his development. Certainly, I can note his triumph over the forces of chaos as Leviathan/Tiamat, but what we do not have is a ruling deity who embodies purely benefic qualities. A solution may be found in considering Azazel, the strong god, as the personification of the unbridled aspect of the storm god; as the fierce shadow cast by Yahweh. Lucifer is then rightly identified with Azazel, standing at the very point where the chasm of dualism yawns into existence.

I propose that, rather than two competing deities, Yahweh and Aza(z)el, we have two names for equal and distinct aspects of one deity. Perhaps this is a cogent explanation for the parity that they are accorded in Leviticus. Thus, my solution to the controversy is that Azazel was originally synonymous with Yahweh: in one tradition God finds his home in the Temple, in the other – arguably pre-exilic – tradition, he is to be found in the wilderness. Therefore, the ritual of atonement enfolds both conceptions of God, one predominantly textual and one oral; one that venerated the tabernacle and the other that still apprehended God as immanent in the wilderness and upon the mountain. Here are two phases of the same religion: one nomadic, which harks back to the desert of Exodus and Moses; the other, that has settled, and in doing so internalised the contradictory idea of the desert as the home of hostile spirits. Furthermore, the division occurs within the psyche – Azazel fated to be not just misunderstood, but demonised in ways that were unimaginable to the nomadic adherents of this semitic cult. The Temple has triumphed over the wild, and the denizens of the mountains and deserts – whether animal, human or spirit – are viewed with increasing suspicion, even hatred.

Having identified the subject, we should turn our attention to the ritual of atonement itself and examine it in context. It is not an innovation, but patterned upon a similar set of rituals common throughout the region. The Hittites, for example, would crown a ram with colourful wool and send it forth to an enemy land to carry away the plague.[3] Other regional scapegoat rituals employ a woman, rather than a goat. A biblical example is given in Numbers 25, in which the Midianite woman is murdered; the terms used to describe the act of killing are those of the offering of a sacrifice. Another Hittite ritual describes how a woman transfers the evil onto a mouse, which is then released. A comparable piece of folk magic is related in 1 Samuel 6, wherein the Philistines make images of golden mice and their buboes,[4] to counter the outbreak of plague provoked by their capture of the Israelites' sacred Ark. The mouse or rat – many languages do not distinguish between the two – is an intermediary between the plague (spirit) and the people. It is a symbol and signifier of contagion, famine and disease. The mouse is also an analogue of the dead, and an image of the soul or double.[5] Much has been made of its ability to access sealed spaces, its squeaking voice, shadowy flitting and supernatural abundance. Mice appear en masse, as the dead are wont to do, and are a sign of imminent disaster: the grain is spoiled, the body corrupts.

Following the trail of seeds stolen from the granary, we note that the mouse was associated with the Mesopotamian Nergal, the originally solar god of epidemics and warfare, and ruler, alongside Ereškigal, of the netherworld. It has been suggested that Nergal stands behind the later Greek Apollo, of the plague-bearing arrows. This latecomer to Olympus was called Aplu by the Hittites and Hurrians, which is Akkadian for 'son' and an epithet of Nergal himself. The earliest form of Apollo seems to have been Apollo Smintheus, often translated as 'mouse,' though it may simply refer to the town of Sminthos. Though the chain Nergal-Aplu-Apollo Smintheus cannot be definitively proven, the similarities between them are striking. Furthermore, these attributes are related to those of Lucifer: light; plague (hence, healing); rulership of the underworld; and, of course, our companion the mouse, which is the most common offering to Lucifer in the grimoire tradition. Even Agrippa lists mice as, 'monstrous beasts... which sometimes are generated by coition, sometimes of the putrefaction of the earth.'[6] Whilst it would be overstating the case to suggest that Lucifer is Nergal or Apollo, nonetheless they are predecessors with whom he bears comparison.

The plague and healing aspect are often overlooked in the Lucifer mythos. The Summer solstice Sun is no longer associated with the fear of disease and plagues of mice that haunted the grain stores of the ancient world. The Devil was, however, linked to disease in the medieval and early modern periods, with the ravages of the Black Death and the attendant claims of witchcraft and poisoning of wells. In gilding the vision of Lucifer with light, it is important not to exclude the vector of contagion, and with it the art of healing.

I will provide a final example of the ritual form of scapegoating, one which has bearing upon our understanding of Babalon: the Hittites would seal images or offerings into lead containers and place them in enemy territory. In an analogous rite, recorded in Zechariah 5:5–11, a woman called 'Wickedness' is discovered in such a vessel and thence carried away by winged women to Babylon, thus removing the sins of Judah. Those familiar with the creation myth of the *Lemegeton,* and the sealing of the spirits in the brazen vessel, may be struck by this parallel. She is the wicked woman evoked in the vision of Revelation 17.[7]

To close, the ritual of atonement is designed to carry the sins of the people into the desert. It is propitiatory and cleansing. It is a sacrifice that replaces a human offering, which was once the king, and/or a priestess or woman. Azazel is not initially a demon, but, as I have proposed above, the 'fierce shadow' of Yahweh. Azazel would become confounded with the idea of sin (especially lust and rebellion), and the goat offering itself. The fall of the goat was, through the exegetic process, bound to the fall of Hêlēl Ben Šaḥar. This identification was hastened by comparative readings of other texts, specifically the extensive Enochic material, and a snarl of politico-religious agendas. We may conjecture that the Deuteronomists considered the rite to preserve the divine aspect of kingship that they sought to excise; but Azazel gained an independent life of his own, the shadow tore free. With the rise of asymmetric dualism, the nomadic memory of the desert deity was lost, to leave only a strictly demonic opposer.

Though the goat was already an emblem of lust in the ancient world, it is after the Azazel of Leviticus, and the *seirim*, that the portrait of the Devil becomes goatish. He is the incarnation of a masculine fleshly desire.[8] Azazel was integrated into a burgeoning demonology that endures in the grimoire tradition. Eventually Christianity unleashed a terror of its own, finding a new enemy in the body of the witch who worships the goat on the high places of the earth. The parable of the sheep and the goats in Matthew 25:31–46 is notable in developing this symbol, but behind this stands the legacy of Leviticus and the sin offering, its horns bound with crimson thread.

The Serpent in the Garden

I have shown that the fall of Hêlêl in Isaiah was a parable on the limits
of divine kingship, rather than an explanation for the existence of
evil in the world. But it would subsequently be read, in conjunction
with Genesis, as part of the process of the personification of evil. It
seems self-evident that a fall is described in Genesis, of man from his
heavenly estate, when Eve is seduced by the serpent into eating of
the tree of knowledge and sharing the forbidden fruit with Adam.
Few realise that this is a Christian reading and is not how the text
would have originally been interpreted. Our understanding is the
fruit of Augustine's fourth century doctrine of Original Sin, which
built on Paul's pronouncement in Romans 5:12, 'Wherefore, as by
one man sin entered into the world, and death by sin; and so death
passed upon all men, for that all have sinned.' Given the methodology by which scripture is interrogated and generated in a process of
repetition and permutation, the cast of Genesis was married with
the Hêlêl of Isaiah and the Azazel of Leviticus. When the Bible is
accepted as the word of God entire, exegesis is tasked with demon-
strating its unity: the serpent in the garden is, along with the goat
and angel, the zoomorphic trope for Lucifer.[1]

The Christian reading adjures us to cover our genitals and feel
shame, with the heretical or gnostic reflex that the Devil/serpent is

the liberator from these bonds.[2] The serpent, an icon of uninhibited sexual expression, is rendered pathological in the new interpretation. The ophidian aspect is coupled with the goat to form a lewd allegory. Such a charismatic, hybrid figure is needed to potentise the ritual transgression of witches' sabbat and Black Mass. But to leap across history to secret conclaves fomenting rebellion is premature; first, there is a nightside of Eden to explore, a drama in the garden where the actions of the protagonists betray an earlier story, or set of stories.

Genesis is a complex text containing demonstrably repurposed Mesopotamian mythemes. The serpent, as symbol of knowledge, became, inevitably, the hero of gnostic readings, with the oft repeated kabbalistic proof that both שהנ 'serpent' and משיח 'messiah' have the same numerical value: 358. The doctrines of the Ophites and Sethians are important clues to the origins of the Genesis story, and indeed hark back to Mesopotamia. Thanks are due to the Church Fathers who gave their version of these 'heresies' and in doing so, engraved them on enduring stone. Epiphanius (320–403 CE) describes the eucharist of the Ophites in some detail in his *Panarion*,[3] in which the worship of the Serpent as God is described as a female-gendered crime, 'He always makes his approach to the feminine whims, pleasures and lusts – in other words to the effeminate ignorance in men...'[4] Epiphanius then proceeds to the ritual, which I will quote in full as it gives rare details of the gnostic version of the fall and their celebration of the sacrament:

It is said that Ialdabaoth did not want men to remember the Mother on high and the Father. But the serpent persuaded them and gave them knowledge, and taught the man and the woman all the mysteries of the heavens. His Father Ialdabaoth, angered that knowledge had been imparted to humankind hurled him down from heaven. For this reason, those who possess the serpent's part, and nothing else, call the serpent 'king of heaven.' Therefore they glorify him for this knowledge, they say, and offer him bread. Indeed they keep a live snake and keep it in a kind of basket. When it is time for their mysteries they take it out of its hiding place, put loaves on the table and call the snake; when the basket is opened it comes out. And thus the snake, which has grown deceitful and cunning, as is its nature, and knows how foolish they are – climbs on to the table and writhes over the loaves. They say that this is the perfect sacrifice. And so – I have been told – not only do they break the loaves touched by the snake's writhing body and offer them to those who are to eat them, but each one of them kisses the snake. The snake has been tamed, either by a magic spell, or placated for the purposes of trickery by some other work of the devil. Yet they worship this creature and call the bread consecrated by its writhing body 'the eucharist.' And they sing a hymn to the father in heaven – once again through the snake, as they say – and thus conlcude their mysteries.[5]

This fascinating account is confirmed by Irenaeus who adds that the divine serpent is a tool of the Mother which, having imparted knowledge, goes on to inspire Cain to murder Abel. The fratricide has become a motif in modern witchcraft traditions to glyph initiation. This does not connote a linear historical survival of the gnostic tradition, as has at times been implied; it is no more than an apposite tale.[6] But we see ostensibly the trappings of the mystery cults, and a mass, which will take the form of the sabbat in the folk practice of Europe.

Irenaeus relates that the serpent was called Michael and Samael, an example of the competing polarities that characterised the gnostic vision. The Ophites (and Peratae) made a further connection with the brazen serpent of Moses, and thus the teaching of magic. As a result they pursued Chaldean science, the arts forbidden by the tyrannical creator Ialdabaoth. Evidently, the gnostics preserved earlier strata of beliefs and practices, even as they turbulently created new and radical approaches to scripture; a discourse fuelled by the Enochian literature and which, in turn, influenced texts such as Revelation.

It is worth stressing how difficult it is to make general statements about the gnostics: the heresiarchs disagree among themselves, as do their polemicists. Irenaeus portrays the serpent as distinct from Christ, Epiphanius as identified with him. Some Ophites venerated the serpent, others saw him as the Enemy. The condemnation of the Gnostics fed into emergent ideas about the congruence of Lucifer, serpent and devil. Their polemics would be used to demonise future heresies, and as the raw material mined in the fabrication of evidence against those who were christened enemies of Church and State. To make the God of Genesis a 'good god,' the sacred serpent, (which was the primary form of the young god and his metastases, both as ruler in the underworld and as healer), had to be 'satanised.'

The vexed relationship with these symbols is further played out in those magical gems upon which the lion-headed serpent Chnoubis/ Chnoumis is depicted. Chnoubis is one of the 36 Egyptian decans, his form very close to that in which the supreme god of certain gnosticising sects was conceived. He was almost certainly identified with the Egyptian creator god Chnum, who resided over the life-giving inundation of the Nile, and further conflated with Yahweh. Signified with the *charakter SSS*, which bears a resemblance to the 666 of Revelation 13:18,[7] Chnoubis and his sign were primarily utilised in amulets for the stomach and the womb. These are predominantly engraved on emerald green stones, including green jasper, agate and heliotrope,[8] a fact that leads me to posit that one etiology for the green stone of Lucifer is to be sought in the widespread use of these amulets (Chnoubis was one of the most frequently depicted figures) in the syncretic period of Late Antiquity. The heliotrope remains intrinsic to goetic magic to this day, its presence in the grimoires attesting to a continuity of practice.

Attilio Mastrocinque, whose *From Jewish Magic to Gnosticism* is the source for much of this information, succinctly explains how Chnoubis was demonised, '...this reversal was a result of Christianization, which clashed with Jewish thinking and the ideas of peoples influenced by Judaism who revered the lion-serpent as a manifestation of the Hebrew god. Christian Gnosticism identifies Chnoubis with the devil, the beast of the apocalypse, whereas doctrines similar

to Gnosticism which remained faithful to Egyptian Judaism continued to revere that divinity.' This demonisation by the Christians was
extended to all divine snakes.

In his *Against Heresies*,[9] Irenaeus describes a further sect, the
Barbelo-Gnostics, who venerated Sophia as the serpent teacher of
gnosis:

> Such are the opinions which prevail among these persons, by
> whom, like the Lernaean hydra, a many-headed beast has been
> generated from the school of Valentinus. For some of them assert
> that Sophia herself became the serpent; on which account she
> was hostile to the creator of Adam, and implanted knowledge in
> men, for which reason the serpent was called wiser than all others.
> Moreover, by the position of our intestines, through which the
> food is conveyed, and by the fact that they possess such a figure,
> our internal configuration in the form of a serpent reveals our
> hidden generatrix.[10]

The female gendering of the serpent could represent a vestige of
its original identity in Genesis being uncannily preserved in some
gnostic traditions.

In the orthodox reading, the serpent of Genesis is a creation of
God, who offers freedom of choice. In this first instance, there is no
conception of an equal and independent evil that opposes the will
of God. The serpent is his creation and, though condemned, is not a
rival with whom Yahweh is locked in unending struggle.

Monotheism always faces the difficult question of the nature of
evil, which must be considered as part of God's plan. It is stated
plainly in Isaiah 45:7, 'I form the light, and create darkness: I make
peace, and create evil: I the Lord do all these things.' These themes
are explored in Job, with the trials that beset the righteous man
who struggles to understand the nature of God. Divine wisdom is
ultimately shown to be unknowable, in the remarkable passages
of Job 38–42. Yet such stoicism is hard to maintain in the face of
the disasters that befall the faithful, and inevitably, strategies are

interjected to distance the omnipotent God from the suffering that occurs under his watch; this is the secret door through which dualism enters the body of the church. A figure is given the lonely task of shouldering the sin burden, silently invited to sit at the back of the congregation, and harangued from the pulpit. In the search for a specific text that promotes this, 1 Chronicles 21:1 must be cited. Chronicles attributes evil to Satan, not to God, in its revisionary telling of Samuel and Kings.

The Christian demonisation of all divine serpents augured a war to be waged upon the entire religio-social order of paganism and the rooting out of cults of great antiquity. Primary amongst these was the cult of Asclepius, a divine healer with near identical qualities to the Christian saviour, but whose symbol was the serpent entwined staff. Asclepius, like Christ, was often figured as a beautiful child, he was a man raised to the status of a god, and died for seeking to save mankind. The crime of Asclepius was resurrecting the dead, which overstepped the permissible boundaries of man, and saw him struck down by a lightning bolt hurled by Zeus. The Christian polemicists drew comparison with Luke 10:18.

The Christian cult deliberately transferred the attribution of the cures of Asclepius to Jesus: for instance, the sick man at Bethesda, who picks up his bed and walks in John 5 and Mark 2:12, is a miracle which actually occurs at an asclepeion. In Revelation 2:12–13, writing to the seven churches, John describes Pergamon as 'Satan's seat.' It is to the great altar to Zeus that he alludes, now at the Pergamon Museum in Berlin, (which, coincidentally, houses the Ishtar Gate). The further reason for this vituperation is the nearby presence of a renowned asclepeion. John indicates this in 2:17; though the allusion is unfamiliar to most modern readers of the Bible, to his contemporaries the image would have been plain, '...and will give him a white stone, and in the stone a new name written, which no man knoweth saving he that receiveth it.' The white stone refers to the tokens left at asclepeia by those who had been healed.[11]

The church consistently attacked the rival healer and divine physician in the sermons and screeds of the Church Fathers. Being unable to dispute the miraculous healings that occured in the sleep chambers, they argued that Christ cured the soul, whereas Asclepius 'only' cured the body. Their perverse logic is shown in the works of Justin Martyr (100–165 CE). In his *First Apology* he acknowledges the similarities between Christ and Asclepius:

> and when we say that He [Christ] healed the lame, the paralytic, and those born blind, and raised the dead, we appear to say things similar to those said to have been done by Asclepius.[12]

But his ultimate conclusion was that Christ as Logos predates the pagan divinities, was prophesied in the Old Testament and therefore cannot be a follower of Asclepius:

> And when he [the devil] brings forward Asclepius as the raiser of the dead and healer of all diseases, may I not say that in this matter likewise he has imitated the prophecies about Christ?[13]

The devil is invoked, but the battle with Asclepius, whose healing cult and hospitals were so esteemed, was not to be easily won. In Late Antiquity (300–600 CE), Asclepius was considered greater than Christ, as texts such as the Acts of Pilate demonstrate.

Origen (184–254 CE) continued the emphasis on soul healing, and perhaps from this talk of 'Christ physician' we can extrapolate future attacks on those who provided rival folk medicine:

> But he who ultimately discovers that Christ has a medicine for souls, will find from these books which are read in the churches, as he finds from mountains and fields, that each yields healing herbs, at least strength won from words, so that any weakness of soul is healed not so much by leaf and bark as by an inward virtue and justice.[14]

Tertullian (160–225 CE) goes further, denouncing Asclepius as 'a beast' and 'a bastard.' He paints the opponents of Christ, the healers

and their patrons, as in league with demons. In his *Apology* we get
a sense of the threatening nature of the universe the Christian cult
felt itself beseiged by:

> We are instructed, moreover, by our sacred books how from
> certain angels, who fell of their own free-will, there sprang a more
> wicked demon-brood, condemned of God along with the authors
> of their race, and that chief we have referred to [Satan]. It will
> for the present be enough, however, that some account is given
> of their work. Their great business is the ruin of mankind. So,
> from the very first, spiritual wickedness sought our destruction.
> They inflict, accordingly, upon our bodies diseases and other
> grievous calamities, while by violent assaults they hurry the soul
> into sudden and extraordinary excesses. Their marvellous subtle-
> ness and tenuity give them access to both parts of our nature. As
> spiritual, they can do no harm; for, invisible and intangible, we
> are not cognizant of their action save by its effects, as when some
> inexplicable, unseen poison in the breeze blights the apples and
> the grain while in the flower, or kills them in the bud, or destroys
> them when they have reached maturity; as though by the tainted
> atmosphere in some unknown way spreading abroad its pestilen-
> tial exhalations.[5]

As the demons spread disease, those who cure are their dupes, and
the medicines simply proxy. Only the word of Christ can bring true
healing, which is not of the body, but of the soul.

By the fourth century, churches were built on the razed foundations of the asclepeia, notably in Epidauros, the omphalos of the
Greek healing complex; in Pergamon, where the the healing spring
was occulted by the baptismal font; and on the island in the Tiber
at Rome. Though this was not the end of the cult of Asclepius, as
evinced by ongoing attacks in the work of Ambrose (340–397 CE)
and Augustine (354–430 CE). Some heresies die harder than others,
but the current ignorance of Asclepius shows that the victory was
won, the sleep chambers a now forgotten dream.

Asclepius, with his serpent wand, is a successor of Ningišzida and the healer gods, amongst whom must be counted the Rephaim. In considering the ophidian aspect of Lucifer, these are important influences and must be reckoned with. The serpent served as the embodied spirit of the ancestral dead. Attacks on the serpent cults were, therefore, an attack on the history and meaning of people, whom, when stripped of their familial and cultural identities, would be better assimilated into the imperial monocult.

It is often assumed that the serpent is strictly phallic, but this is an injustice to its polyvalent nature, which encircles a female aspect. As such, amongst its myriad guises, the serpent is also an epiphany of the chthonic chaos goddess of prehistory. The dread figures of Lotan, Leviathan and Tiamat come to mind; indeed, they are summoned from the depths of memory in Revelation 12 and 20, chapters that do double duty, serving additionally to polemicise Sethian and Ophite doctrine. In this context they are presented as male and equated with Satan, yet the great Red Dragon which casts forth the flood from its mouth is an antediluvian menstrual motif. With this understanding, access is granted to a primal stratum of symbolism in Genesis, which is rarely discussed: namely, the association of the serpent with the cult of the ophidian goddess Ašerah, and the earliest beliefs of the ancient Israelites. Occultists are often familiar with the gnostic idea of the serpent as *soteiros*, a continuation of the Mesopotamian healing cults. I aim here to restore the pre-Christian and pre-Jewish reading.

Genesis was one of the texts crafted by the Deuteronomists, whose agenda, as I have shown, opposed divine kingship. In Genesis 3 another set of symbols are employed with the same end in mind: the serpent and the tree; symbols that can be read as serving a narrative which rejects human sacrifice, divine kingship (as exemplified by Solomon), and the concealed consort of Yahweh, Ašerah. This is not apparent on the first reading, as the references to cultic symbols are not part of our koiné, and thus require some elucidation for the modern reader.

In the Bible, Ašerah is either a goddess or a pole, pale or stick, which caused much confusion in early scholarship; the debate exploited by those who sought to deny that there was such a goddess. This was settled by the discovery of the Ugaritic Baal texts, which provided evidence that the the cult statue (the poles were carved) and the goddess are inseparable. The *ašerah* itself, as a cultic repository of force, may well be related to the fiery contagion of the thyrsus of Dionysos, and the caduceus,[16] which combines the serpent(s) and the tree into a composite and sexualised form.[17]

Ašerah is one of several ophidian goddesses found in the region. Certainly, Ašerah, Ištar and Astarte were transposable by the fourteenth century BCE, and each intimately associated with the serpent. To this list I can further add the Phoenician Tanit and the Egyptian Qudšu, who was depicted as a naked woman standing on a lion holding serpents and lotus flowers. In the opinion of scholar Leslie S. Wilson, who has forensically examined the Hebrew:

> Both ᾿TRT and Qudšu became assimilated into Israelite cult worshipped as Ašerah and the Hebrew Qadesh respectively. The former became the focus of all things evil while the latter entered the language of the Israelites as the reviled cultic prostitute.[18]

Genesis 3 reads very differently in this light. The serpent, fondly associated with Lucifer – due in large part to the Midrash which projects the fallen angel characters of Azazel and Samael back onto it – conceals a goddess whose existence and rites were anathema to the Deuteronomists.

Increasingly, the evidence shows that Ašerah was the consort of Yahweh. In spite of ongoing attempts to destroy the artefacts that bear witness to this divine marriage, instigated by the political and religious interests that govern Israel, a vista opens up revealing an Israelite religion that grew out of Canaanite cults; a religion which continued to blend Yahwism with pagan practice until the Deuteronomist reforms. Even when the material evidence is compromised, the text testifies to the importance of the goddess to the early Israelite peoples.

Eve is not tempted by a male serpent, but is initiated by the goddess Ašerah, garbed in serpent form – who is also understood to be the tree.[19] Eve in turn initiates Adam, and has been consistently identified as the first witch ever since.[20] In backlighting scripture, the concealed text of Genesis is read as an attack on the original form of Israelite religion, and the very existence of a goddess. As the memory of the source and matrix of the religion was destroyed, the story was freed to take on a new meaning, with the devil drafted in as arch seducer.

If the target of the Deuteronomists is the worship of Ašerah, the same story can also be used to deny divine kingship, the form of rulership that is contingent upon the goddess. These are both halves of the same apple. Thus the text can be read allegorically, to explain Adam's fall from the state of 'David' to that of the apostate 'Solomon,' and his expulsion from Eden. Those unused to the initiatic reading of myth may struggle to understand how Adam can be both David and Solomon, but the unity of father and son (or brothers) as contrasting halves of a single entity, is a common symbolic technique.[21] Eve too, in this elucidation, is both serpent goddess and her daughter, the first woman whose name appropriately means 'life.' Her name in Hebrew is חוה (Ḥavvah), derived from the root חיה (ḥwy), to live, to exist.[22] The striking similarity to Aramaic ḥewya' and the Arabic ḥayya, which mean 'serpent' – conveying the hidden meaning of the mother of life – has been noted.

I would conjecture that eating the 'apple,' most likely the fruit of the mandrake, is a sign that they were assenting to sexual union. Furthermore, the fruit, flowers and root of the mandrake belong to the complex of symbola surrounding the sacred marriage of king and goddess, from which kingship derives its authority. Eve offers the fruit to Adam: it is the woman who initiates. The matrilineal conception is a sign of its antiquity. Yet, patriarchy has consistently derided as sexual 'weakness' the abundant desires of Eve; this fable misused to reinforce an assumed male dominance. Every woman, as a daughter of Eve, is made to feel shame for her sexual jouissance, for her body as desire incarnate; and this excess is one of the primary explanations for witchcraft in the European witch panic.[23]

The aphrodisiac scent of the mandrake fruit is conveyed in the lush eroticism of the Song of Songs, pseudepigraphically ascribed to Solomon. The Hebrew ברא (*bara*), meaning fire, is an alternate name of mandrake,[24] which recalls that the serpent was anciently thought to be the seed of fire, containing the properties of venom, contagion, healing and the heat of passion. The mandrake is a symbolon of the evening star, and the rising of Sirius, as the description of Josephus obliquely alludes to, in a passage drawing on Solomonic lore and the magical practice of the time:

> [I]ts colour is like to that of flame, and towards the evenings it sends out a certain ray like lightning. It is not easily taken by such as would do it, but recedes from their hands, nor will yield itself to be taken quietly, until either the urine of a woman, or her menstrual blood, be poured upon it; nay, even then it is certain death to those that touch it, unless any one take and hang the root itself down from his hand, and so carry it away. It may also be taken another way, without danger, which is this: they dig a trench quite round about it, till the hidden part of the root be very small, they then tie a dog to it, and when the dog tries hard to follow him that tied him, this root is easily plucked up, but the dog dies immediately, as if it were instead of the man that would take the plant away; nor after this need any one be afraid of taking it into their hands. Yet, after all this pains in getting, it is only valuable on account of one virtue it hath, that if it be only brought to sick persons, it quickly drives away those called demons, which are no other than the spirits of the wicked, that enter into men that are alive and kill them, unless they can obtain some help against them.[25]

The unexpurgated translation, which I've quoted here in full, includes the detail of urine or menstrual blood, often omitted for the sake of decency. Josephus chooses to remain silent on the erotic magical uses of the plant, neglecting both the perfume and the flesh of the 'apple' and the ritual use of a philtre obtained by steeping its root in wine. The use of a similar psychoactive beverage in the hieros gamos is attested in our earliest surviving mythological narrative,[26] impressed in cuneiform in the Early Dynastic III period. The narrative recounts the wandering of the solar hero Lugalbanda through the eastern mountains, in which liminal setting he meets a goddess, Ninsumun/Ninsun.[27] She offers him to drink of the *agarin*, a kind of beer potentised with mandrake and belladonna, their eyes become dazed and thus intoxicated they consumate their union. As with the initiatic dynamic between Eve and Adam, it is Ninsun who is described as knowing 'great things,' and it is Lugalbanda who comes to know, experiencing a 'great light,' as a result of partaking of the sacrament with the goddess.[28] The obverse of the tablet describes the subsequent necromantic ritual in which a priestess of Inanna is summoned to prophesy on the fruit of their loins.

Perhaps with this understanding of the Eden myth, and its sacramental rites, it is possible to recapture the original meaning of the polemic, rather than grafting our modern preoccupations onto it. Stated simply, Eve as the serpent goddess gifts sexual knowledge and bestows kingship. It is she who initiates Adam into these mysteries. In this way, the origin myth of witchcraft begins: in the swelling poison from that rapid slap of a bite, the fire that courses in the sap of the holy tree, the spinal marrow writhing up from sacrum to skull; it is the aphrodisiac love gift bestowed by the evening star; it is sex, and self-knowledge.

Ašerah may seem distant to us, but when we turn to our working texts, in particular the *Lemegeton* or *Lesser Key*, we find this written of Astaroth:

> The 29th spirit in order is Named Astaroth, he is a Mighty & strong duke, & appeareth in [the] form of an unbeautifull angel, ridding on an Infernal like dragon, and carrying in his right hand a viper (you must not lett him come to neare y^u least he doe y^u damage by his stinking Breath.) Therefore ye Exorcist must hold ye Magicall Ring nere to his face and y^t will defend him he giveth true answares of things present past & to come & can discover all

secreets; he will declare willingly how yᵉ spirits fell, if desired, & yᵉ reason of his own fall. He can make men wounderfull knowing in all Liberall siences; he rules 40 Legions of spirits, his seal is as this [shown], wᶜʰ weare as a Lamen before yᵘ, or else he wⁱˡˡ not obey you.[29]

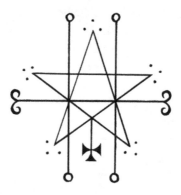

Without giving a full exegesis on this spirit and her signature, the salient features can still be extracted. Firstly, that this is the demon-ised Ašerah, complete with serpents; secondly, that the seal contains a mandrake in the form of the pentagram,[30] behind the barred gates to Eden; thirdly, that the fall is explicated in her powers; and finally, that there is a European grimoire tradition that has consistently engaged with her as one of its principal spirits. She is Astaroth, who is legitimately Inanna, Ištar, Astarte, and the Cyprian Aphrodite, whose DNA luminesces in the vision of Revelation as the Whore of Babylon.[31]

We see through the Middle Ages the serpent of Eden depicted not as a male Satan, nor an androgyne, but as a woman with flowing hair and bare breasts: a tantalising iconographic continuity that is also beheld in the related Melusine legends. Our supposedly late and cor-rupt traditions contain numerous curious elements that lead those who work with these intelligences to posit their enduring presence with us in the journey of our species from dawn to gathering dusk.

Fall and Flood

Often missed in the reading of Genesis is a second fall, which follows the sin of Adam and Eve – the final vector that intersects with Isaiah and Leviticus to produce the Lucifer mythos.[1] As I noted in the previous chapter, the transgression of Adam and Eve was not originally held to be the fall. We miss this because we are not familiar with Hebrew and have accepted the cultural meaning imposed on the Old Testament by Christianity. The story of Adam and Eve became the focus of the new religion; partly to distance it from the angelic speculation and discredited texts that were once so important, but had become a breeding ground of heresies.

Sifting through the interminable genealogy of 'begats' in Genesis 5 we discover a clue, not to who fell, but as to when the fall occurred. The genealogy gives Jared as the father of Enoch. The meaning of Jared derives from the root ירד, 'to descend or fall,' directing us to the moment when the primeval fall occurred: within the lifetime of Jared, before the cataclysm of the great flood. The deliberate allusion is repeated and explained in Jubilees 4:15: (italics mine)

and he called his name *Jared*, for in his days the angels of the Lord *descended* on the earth, those who are named the Watchers, that they should instruct the children of men, and that they should do judgment and uprightness on the earth.

The work, obviously heir to an oral tradition, is supplementary to Genesis, and is being explained to a conclave of eager listeners who lack the exegetic skills to extract the meaning of the allusion for themselves.

History is divided by the flood, an event that erased the scribal landscape of the past and consigned the kings and heroes, gods and legends to an inaccessible abode in the cold heavens and name-less graves. Magic has long sought to recover this lost knowledge, something that seemed irretrievable by conventional means. It is the edges of this ur-myth of human history that apocalypticism silvers and Revelation ultimately gilds.

Genesis looks back to the great flood, as an event in prehistory, and imposes upon it a new meaning. The text itself is likely to have been composed just before, or most likely during, the Babylonian exile. The dating seems secure, given the clearly Mesopotamian origins of such key figures as Noah and Enoch. The great flood is recorded in *Atra-Hasis*, with the same episode repeated in the *Epic of Gilgameš* and by Berossus in his lost *Babyloniaca*. These tales are the raw material for Genesis, but the characters that were once foreign become nativised.

The cataclysm was taken as a sign of divine vengeance, and it would inspire the wildest conjecture as to its import. In Genesis, the flood is not the work of the devil, because he did not, at thatpoint, exist. It is the work of an angry god, the reason for whose displeasure must be grasped to formulate the first question: why, according to Genesis, was this devastation unleashed?

Genesis 6 gives God's supposed motives, but it is a difficult pas-sage, as infamous as Isaiah 14, and will likewise need careful analysis. Scripture relates the tale thus:

And it came to pass, when men began to multiply on the face of the earth, and daughters were born unto them; That the sons of

God saw the daughters of men that they were fair; and they took
them wives of all which they chose. And the Lord said, My spirit
shall not always strive with man, for that he also is flesh: yet his
days shall be an hundred and twenty years. There were giants
[Nephilim] in the earth in those days; and also after that, when
the sons of God came in unto the daughters of men, and they bare
children to them, the same became mighty men which were of
old, men of renown. And God saw that the wickedness of man was
great in the earth, and that every imagination of the thoughts of
his heart was only evil continually. And it repented the Lord that
he had made man on the earth, and it grieved him at his heart.

As we have come to expect from our biblical sources, the account
given is terse, unsatisfactory. Major events of profound mythic significance are passed over in a matter of lines. This, in itself, explains
the many variant stories that emerge. Reading the passage again, no
'fall' is described here; neither is there a golden-locked leader of the
angels, nor a description of how many transgress, nor an unequivocal celestial origin for the sons of God. As is so often the case, we
tend to believe we know the story of scripture, but the text reveals
something quite different.

The text of Genesis 6 is not just an etiology for the existence of
giants upon the Earth. Here we have divine beings who couple with
mortal women. The hybrid offspring are semi-divine beings who, as
immortals, embody the fear expressed in Genesis 3:22–24 of those
who have eaten of the tree of life itself: (italics mine)

And the Lord God said, Behold, the man is become as one of us,
to know good and evil: and now, *lest he put forth his hand, and take
also of the tree of life, and eat, and live for ever*: Therefore the Lord God
sent him forth from the garden of Eden, to till the ground from
whence he was taken. So he drove out the man; and he placed at
the east of the garden of Eden Cherubims, and a flaming sword
which turned every way, to keep the way of the tree of life.

From a comparative reading we deduce that God does not wish man to realise his divine nature, or to live beyond his allotted span, a motif found prominently in the *Epic of Gilgameš*. This is the vestige of a very ancient human origin story: the explanation for why we all must die.

Genesis is a complex collection of such founding human myths, an Ark in itself. It seeks to answer the fundamental questions that peoples of all cultures ask themselves: What happened in the creation? Where do we come from? Why do we die? What happened in the ancient past? How should we live? What is the nature of god? What is the nature of man? The way in which these questions and the answers to them are framed can be spun for political, religious and economic ends, but nonetheless preserve the oldest human narratives.[2] In Genesis we have a far from seaworthy text, where the tales, often competing stories, are heaped upon each other, a maritime graveyard foundered on the unmarked reef of pre-history that continues to claim new victims.

Sin is given a sexual connotation in Genesis 6:1–4, with the implication that intermarriage is forbidden. This doubles as a propaganda attack on those who, during the Babylonian exile, did not keep themselves apart. Certainly, the Deuteronomists used it for such an end; however, the deviation of the priest class is not the primary target of this text, though such a reading is frequently assumed. The actions of the daughters of men echo the carnal sin of Eve, but they are not singled out for the transgression; rather, it is man who is to be punished for his inherent wickedness. Genesis is unsatisfactory in the terse account it gives. Surely it would make more sense if the flood was aimed at the giants? Yet, very evidently in the Genesis account, the flood neither wipes out the giants, nor the Sons of God – for that version of the catastrophe, as one which obliterates the divine beings, we will have to look to Enoch. The target for destruction is 'man,' as we read in Genesis 6:7:

And the Lord said, I will destroy man whom I have created from the face of the earth; both man, and beast, and the creeping thing, and the fowls of the air; for it repenteth me that I have made them.[3]

According to Genesis 8:21: the imagination of man's heart is evil from his youth. For this reason, humankind is fated to be destroyed. A deeply pessimistic view of man as subject to the dictates of divine law; a law against which he must not rebel, in return for God staying his hand and never again unleashing disaster upon him.

The survival of the semi-divine beings is attested, and we can infer that it was they who went on to build the tower of Babel in Genesis 11:1–9. Nimrod is given, by tradition, as the architect of the tower,[4] and is described in Genesis 10:9 as a 'mighty hero,' גִּבֹּר (gibbor), the exact term used for the progeny of the 'fallen' angels. Whilst it is possible that the original intention of the flood story was to account for the destruction of these demi-gods, this is not what Genesis relates; nor can it explain the giants who we encounter time and again in the Bible, most famously in the story of David and Goliath.[5]

Can we take this text at face value, as an account of sexual union between divine beings and mortal women, who give birth to prodigies? Or should we be more cautious in our approach? In order to continue I need to make clear who our protagonists are. Genesis 6 is ambiguous in that it does not say whether the 'sons of god' are the same as the 'mighty men.' The scholarly consensus is that the sons of god mate with the daughters of men who give birth to mighty men. The mighty men are, of course, the Nephilim, often given in translation as giants.

It is tempting to assume that the sons of god are fallen angels.[6] However, in Genesis there is no indication that this is the case. The author does not narrate a particular myth here, such as Gilgameš, but gives the general conception of divine beings consorting with mortal women to describe the disorder before the flood. When read in conjunction with Isaiah, and through the filter of the Deuteronomists, it gains a further meaning: an attack on the divine provenance of kingship, with the king as the son of the goddess, whose sons are semidivine heroes.

The 'crime' that can be adduced in Genesis is that the sons of god are not fulfilling their correct role in the heavenly court, that is, of praising the ruling deity. The Old Testament contains traces of the earlier notion of God as belonging to a divine council, the members of which are often described as stars – a Babylonian conception that betrays older stellar cults. The sons of god have not fallen; that reading develops out of the text,[7] and the stories that are told after it, to make sense of the bare bones of Genesis. The ha-Satan of Job, in particular, is conflated with this tale. The divine council are first demonised, then excluded and finally reintroduced in the familiar guise of angels who have lost their volition and merely carry out the orders of the divine dictator: bar one, and his cohorts, who are allotted a different role.

The same process is found in Deuteronomy 4:19, which instructs that God has no countenance, and counsels against the celestial company, 'And lest thou lift up thine eyes unto heaven, and when thou seest the sun, and the moon, and the stars, even all the host of heaven, shouldest be driven to worship them, and serve them, which the Lord thy God hath divided unto all nations under the whole heaven.' The same course as Deuteronomy is seen at a later stage of development in Psalm 82, in which Elohim is given dominion over the entire earth (whereas in Genesis he is *primus inter pares*). Somewhat ironically, the psalm dates from the Babylonian exile, and is typical of the apocalyptic response to crisis: (italics mine)

> God standeth in the congregation of the mighty; he judgeth among the gods.
> How long will ye judge unjustly, and accept the persons of the wicked? Selah.
> Defend the poor and fatherless: do justice to the afflicted and needy.
> Deliver the poor and needy: rid them out of the hand of the wicked.
> They know not, neither will they understand; they walk on in darkness: all the foundations of the earth are out of course.

I have said, Ye are gods; and all of you are children of the most
  High.
But ye shall die like men, and fall like one of the princes.
Arise, O God, judge the earth: for thou shalt inherit all nations.

Of note is the curse heaped upon the stellar company of El Elyon,
that they shall 'fall like one of the princes.' It is a striking image that
I will return to when I discuss Job, in which the Satan is one of the
divine council.

Returning to the cast of Genesis, can we then surmise that the
Nephilim, the divine offspring of mortal women and stellar gods,
are the fallen angels? The etymology suggests it, but if Nephilim
comes from 'to fall,' what does this fall literally mean? J. C. De Moor[8]
suggests nephilim is an Aramaic past participle and could mean 'the
fallen,' that is, those who fell in battle. This concords with the use of
the verb לפנ (naphal), to fall, as in Ezekiel 32:20–27. The fall is therefore not a heavenly event, such as a comet or meteor, but signifies 'to
die.' We should note, however, that the death of a king is presaged in
the heavens and thus the two ideas cannot be entirely sundered. The
fate of the Nephilim is to fall in order to rise as deified stars, exactly
the fate mocked and denied to the king of Babylon in Isaiah. For the
Nephilim to be described as the mighty men, men of renown, only
makes sense if they are the Mighty Dead. These are the ancestral
heroes, the god-men whose death cult was prohibited by the Deuteronomists.

With this understanding, it is appropriate that Nephilim is often
translated as giants – their stature demands it. Yet we do not have
any indication where these giants have come from in the story of
creation. It has been proposed by Bartelmus and Kvanvig[9] that this
part of Genesis is a mythical etiology, a story to explain the origin
of giants and primeval heroes (*gibborim*), and that these stories were
originally used to legitimise ruling dynasties. Power inevitably seeks
divine sanction.

Giant is derived from the Greek γίγαντας (*gigantas*) and means
'born of/from earth.' This has a chthonic connotation; it does not

necessarily imply beings of superhuman size, indeed the giants depicted on Greek vases are warriors in shining bronze helmets and armour. The confusion is found in the Hebrew as well as Greek, where Cyclopean architecture, ancient tombs and previous warrior races are combined into the same category. The sobriquet 'born of earth' is applied to the ghost of Samuel, who is raised by the witch of Endor in the only complete necromantic ritual preserved in the Bible. Samuel, as a prophet and a judge, ranks amongst the Mighty Dead, whom the witch as a ritual specialist is able to summon from Sheol. Therefore, in 1 Samuel 28:13 we read, 'And the king said unto her, Be not afraid: for what sawest thou? And the woman said unto Saul, I saw gods ascending out of the earth.'

In the *Phoenician History* of Philo, the description of giants is a report of the achievement of power in human civilisation; Kvanvig[10] sees the biblical account as serving the same purpose. Such power is matched by dangers, most notably the ambitious rebellion implicit in the raising of the tower of Babel, the building of cities,[11] and the knowledge of metal work leading to the manufacture of the weapons of war. Genesis is, therefore, a dialogue about the agreed limits of human knowledge and power, and it suggests that we are most dangerous when we are most like God. The Nephilim are mighty rulers of divine origin from primeval time, and the compiler(s) of Genesis intends them to be reviled for enabling humans to be more like the creator.

Though this encounter with giants might seem unfamiliar, we have encountered the Nephilim already in our story, guised as the Rephaim. In Numbers 13:33, the descendants of the Nephilim are seen living in Canaan during the time of Moses; here the Nephilim are described as 'sons of Anak.' Then in Deuteronomy 2:10-21, the Anakites are called Rephaim and characterised as giants. We can deduce that Nephilim is equivalent to Rephaim.

To recap, the Rephaim in Isaiah 14 are the dead who greet the 'fallen' king. Now it seems we draw closer to a legitimate understanding of Lucifer. He is fallen, a king in the underworld. 'Oh N.N. how fallen art thou' is the ritual formula of the lament that Isaiah parodies. It must, therefore, be a sorrowful judgement upon our culture that we have popularly identified our ancestors with extraterrestrials[12] rather than the dead who periodically ascend to their stellar abode; having forgotten our origins we interpolate a technological myth that merely speaks of our own isolation from the great river of blood and that great city of dust whose name must not be spoken. The biblical account is conflicted: it cannot give divine status to a rival culture and thus its gods and ancestors become abominations and rebellious angels, as does the company of heaven which once supported Yahweh and his consort.[13]

There is, at heart, a confusion of two stories. One, a myth common in the ancient world, that our race was preceded by a stronger warrior strain of giants whose monuments still stand, with the inference of divine kingship and an ancestral cult. The other is an origin myth for mankind, who though clay born, contains a divine spark. But with this celestial gift comes self-knowledge, inevitable rebellion and deific ire. Julius Wellhausen's oft repeated description of Genesis 6:1–4 as a 'cracked erratic boulder'[14] is well observed, yet I propose a different metaphor: Lucifer is the child of the forked horns of this dilemma of origins, the spark that leaps between them.

In the history of error, I have returned to the Urzeit, the primeval time demarked by the flood, and demonstrated that the Lucifer story was born from the creative conflict of tales thrown together and demanding resolution. We know instinctively that scripture on this matter is severely lacking. I have shown that the Lucifer mythos one would expect to find in Genesis is entirely absent. This has created a dangerous ground that tempts us to project our hopes and fears into a shadowy past that most have only a rudimentary knowledge of. One of the pitfalls of occult approaches to Lucifer has been to rely on the secondary sources regarding the Nephilim and Anunnaki and the sensationalist sophistry of alternative historians, to piece together a narrative from fragments and wild conjecture. I have taken a more pragmatic approach, going to the primary source of Genesis 6:1–4 and to secure scholarly positions in order to create as accurate a picture as is possible.

The giants are the Rephaim, the mighty ancestral dead, and Lucifer primus inter pares in the underworld and heavens. Having disentangled the identities of the characters as they appear in the first book of the Bible and in Canaanite religion, I will now turn to earlier sources: the Mesopotamian texts and traditions that survived the deluge. These cast light on Genesis 6, the deluge and the mythical figures who stand upon the flood plain.

The Key

The flood story is extremely ancient and widespread, dating back to well before the Ice Age.[1] This argues against searching for a specific Near Eastern catastrophic event, as biblical literalists and alternative historians have done. With the true shape of our ancient past emerging we would do well to integrate it into our model rather than relying on the quaint misunderstandings of 'tradition.' Occult science must not merely be superstition, it must seek the light. If there is an existent myth that explains the Nephilim, sons of god, giants and the origin of evil, then this has huge significance for our understanding and, by extension, our practice. I believe that *Atra-Hasis* and the Mesopotamian corpus is demonstrably the missing key that Enoch is often taken for. We should note here that the supposition of Milik, that Enoch predates Genesis, though at one time a beguiling idea has now been entirely disproved.[2]

Atra-Hasis has not impacted on the occult tradition as it was only recently translated by Lambert and Millard (1965) following Laessø's reconstruction of the text in 1956. Millard's subsequent comparison of *Atra-Hasis* with Genesis was only published in 1967.[3]

Further work on the text has resulted in revised versions, most notably in 1996 by A. R. George and F. N. H. Al-Rawi. I must also cite the work of Helge Kvanvig in *Roots of Apocalyptic* and *Primeval History*; both texts have been pivotal to my understanding.

The story of *Atra-Hasis* is straightforward enough to be told and remembered. The three great gods An, Enlil and Enki rule the heavens, earth and the great deep. Beneath them are the seven Anunnaki. Beneath them the Igigu gods labour, tasked with digging the course of the Tigris and Euphrates rivers. The Igigu tire of their lot and rise up, burning their tools in an act of open rebellion. This act of defiance results in the creation of man to do the heavy work that the Igigu gods disdained. In the story, mankind is created from the flesh and blood of the rebel god Geštu-e, mixed with the spittle of the gods. Spit is an important magical fluid in shamanism, less so in modern magic wher,e if it is employed at all, it is only in cursing procedures such as the denial of the cross. The creative aspect of spittle is that it was considered equivalent to sperm. In Sumerian semen/rain/water are the same word; the same is true in Akkadian. The dismemberment of the rebel god in the creation myth of man is eerily similar to the fate of Dionysos at the hands of the Titans (*sparagmos*). It has, in addition, a profound symbolic meaning in the sabbat feast (communion) of witchcraft where the child Lucifer is ritually consumed, and the identities of the participants torn asunder.[4]

Man's creation from the rebel god gifted him a spirit that was both strong and able to scheme, comparable to the more familiar Greek *mētis*.[5] The creation epic *Atra-Hasis* does not make man evil or rely on a devil figure: Geštu-e is fittingly a god of wisdom. The description of him in the rebellion is 'the god who had planning capacity.' The spirit of the rebel god reminds us of the cost of rebellion, we are formed from both his ghost: *etemmu*, and his divine ability to scheme and apply rationality: *tēmu*. A wordplay, that shows each aspect as integral to the other. But we are not simply made from these divine substances; in *Atra-Hasis* we are born of a goddess, something Genesis cannot countenance – though as I have shown in the previous chapter, the evidence has not been entirely effaced.

The creation of mankind in *Atra-Hasis*, based on the metaphor of making clay bricks, is often misleadingly equated with some kind of

DNA experiment. It is a typical error of the technological-salvation-ist interpretation and has no scholarly credibility. Furthermore, it ignores the prevalence of similar creation myths patterned across the globe.

The new humans were designed to do the hard labour of digging irrigation ditches, showing that this the recension of this myth dates to the beginning of agriculture. It is clear that agriculture represents a rift, even a fall; and that it facilitated the rise of the city, which requires a surplus to function.[6] Coexistent with this process, the domestication of animals created a new vector of disease and plague that will have been a disturbing development in human society. Our relation with the city has always been ambivalent. Anarchists, such as Hakim Bey, continue to argue that the city and agriculture created the necessity for slavery. Anarcho-primitivists such as John Zerzan go further, and green anarchists argue that there is no difference between the slavery of animals (domestication) and humans (whether wage or slave labour). All these controversies are already present in *Atra-Hasis*.

The shift to a predominantly sedentary, agrarian culture coincides with the reduced stature of people. This is due to the change in diet to an increased reliance on grain. The difference between these new agriculturalists and the previous hunter/gardeners is perhaps another contributing factor to the idea of an earlier race of giants, as is the survival of their cyclopean monuments as enigmas in the landscape. A more contentious explanation for the giants would be an oral culture's remembrance of Neanderthals, encountered by Homo sapiens sapiens in the Levant, with whom genetic analysis now proves we interbred. Evidence suggests that the offspring of these unions tended to infertility.[7]

The divine aspect of us is evidently the blood, and this is a common thread in mythology. We see it in *Enûma Eliš*, the Sumerian creation myth:

> It was Kingu who contrived the uprising,
> And made Tiamat rebel, and joined the battle;

They bound him, holding him before Ea.
They imposed on him his guilt and severed his blood (veins)
Out of his blood they fashioned mankind...

Berossus explains likewise in his *Babyloniaca*:

This god took off his own head
and the other gods gathered up the blood which flowed from it
and mixed the blood with earth and formed men.
For this reason men are intelligent
and have a share of divine wisdom

Ultimately humans rebel against their yoke, just as the Igigu gods
did against the Anunnaki; and this is as a direct result of the divine
substance from which they have been fashioned. Rebellion is in our
blood. The root of rebellion is *re-bellum*, the renewal of war, and it is
the first conflict that we continue to reenact. In this primal myth it
is clear that men are all 'of the blood,' though people are clearly apportioned *mêtis* in varying degrees. Not everyone is an Odysseus, but
neither are we the scoundrels Genesis would cast us as. The blood is
contagion, spirit, which in another context is what Leviticus tries to
protect against by cutting the throat and bleeding out the sacrifice.[8]
Returning to the narrative of *Atra-Hasis*: the people multiply and
raise a noise which provokes the ire of Enlil. Noise is often taken to
refer to overpopulation, just as in Genesis 6:1. This reading remains
popular as it ties into a narrative based on human overpopulation
degrading the carrying capacity of the environment. Cities require
agriculture which creates a surplus that leads to population growth.
Agriculture is unsustainable, as the yields of the land decrease with
the exhaustion of the soil. Working the land requires slave labour,
the back-breaking digging of irrigation ditches. As the land base is
degraded, wars of conquest are the inevitable result, to feed the cities
and the appetites of their entrenched elites. Those who have read
Apocalyptic Witchcraft will know that this is an argument that I am
sympathetic to, yet here I think it is not nuanced enough.

To truly apprehend what is expressed here, I will examine the nature of the 'noise' which provokes Enlil. In Akkadian a deliberate homonym is employed to show the relationship and indivisibility of these two qualities: noise and rebellion. The noise is a cry of despair arising from travail and of hunger, which becomes a cry of rebellion. The same complaint of noise is repeated in *Erra and Išum*, in which Marduk is the source of retribution:

> Let them go beside you, when the clamor of human habitations becomes noisome to you,
> And you resolve to wreak destruction...

We are impelled to rebel because we contain an imperishable element of divinity. The Yahwist who composed Genesis would prefer us to believe that this quality is 'wickedness.' But, as Finkelstein[9] points out, 'noise' is found in Genesis 18:20–21 in relation to the outcry in Sodom. Noise and rebellion are synonymous.[10]

We can go deeper than that, for the same complaint is present in Genesis 6:3, a line whose complexity is not apparent in the KJV translation, 'And the Lord said, My spirit shall not always strive with man, for that he also is flesh: yet his days shall be an hundred and twenty years.'

It says on the surface what would be expected: that our mortal span has been ordained by god, that spirit and flesh are distinct, one is eternal and one finite. But the text contains two difficult words, neither of which is known in Hebrew: *yādōn* and *šagam*. Yādōn is glossed in the KJV as 'strive,' but is more likely to derive from an Akkadian root meaning 'to be strong.' This makes sense, and is a better fit than the ambivalent rendering of 'strive.' The second word, šagam, is entirely concealed in the KJV, lost in translation, glossed as 'for that he,' its meaning construed as 'because'; this seems logical, as flesh does not endure whilst God does. However, such a translation is an impossibility. The root *šgm* is also found in Akkadian, the language of *Atra-Hasis*. As a verb it means 'to howl, roar, cry, shout' and as a noun 'loud cry, noise.' The underlying meaning of the line should therefore be read as follows, 'My spirit shall not be powerful in man for everlasting time on account of the noise.'

The subtext of Genesis 6:3 is now apparent: it is telling the same story as *Atra-Hasis*. Humankind is clamorous because it contains within it a divine and powerful spirit. Somewhat troublingly for Judaism, it is not necessarily the spirit of God, but of the rebel. This is the heresy of Lucifer. Humanity is created in the likeness of the gods, but in *Atra-Hasis* it requires the intercession of the rebel god to bring us consciousness. This gift of knowledge is bought at the price of death. In Genesis, the rebel god is in the first instance, the goddess, guised as a serpent. The first humans are expelled from the garden of Eden to wander the world and commit the sins of agriculture, animal domestication and the building of cities. Cain is a vital figure in this history. Yet it is noteworthy that there is no single account of the gaining of knowledge. The serpent and tree episode is followed by the sexual congress of women with angels/sons of god. Both glyph the attainment of knowledge, both relate it to a carnal transmission. Thus the gibborim and the primeval man, Adam, can be seen as parallel mythic figures. Both are animated by the divine spirit. Understand that the idea explored in Genesis is accomplished by recording variants of the same human story. The account of creation likewise preserves contradictory variants. Genesis is a palimpsest of the traditions of the antediluvian scribes.

To précis, the serpent story is both a rememberance of divine kingship and a polemic against the goddess. The fallen angels story is a version of the *Atra-Hasis* myth of the rebel god whose blood is the equivalent of the venom and apple of Ašerah. The two stories are combined in the process of exegesis. By extension, the serpent can now be equated securely with the viperish sons of god, and their leader in particular, whom, as I have noted, is absent in Genesis – but not in the allied Enochian traditions. Logic indicates that the existence of the serpent requires an equivalent figure to appear in the daughters of men/sons of god cross-matching. It is the Enochian literature that performs this act of magic. Lucifer steps into the ambiguous role of the rebel god in the tailoring of Isaiah, but with an origin in Genesis and, in the beginning, *Atra-Hasis*.

Practically, this indicates two distinct ritual approaches, that of Adam, and that of the daughters of men. I have demonstrated that both contain the same elements, despite outward differences: sexual initiations from spirits which have a markedly ophidian character.

To return again to *Atra-Hasis*, the Akkadian words that describe the causes of the flood are *rigmu* and *ḫuburu*. Rigmu is often used as a metaphor for the thunder of Adad, as is *sagāmu*, and means 'to cry out, scream, voice.' Elsewhere in *Atra-Hasis* it is unequivocally 'a war cry.' Therefore we have two linked concepts, those of despair and rebellion. Rigmu is given to man at his creation, with these implicit and insoluble qualities. Hūburu is, for the most part, translated as 'uproar.' Enlil complains about these as causes, not 'increase,' leading Kvanvig to surmise that population growth is not the core issue, but employed in the narrative to explain the increasing tumult. The gods respond to the crisis of noise with plague, drought, famine and, ultimately, flood. But Atrahasis, the eponymous flood hero, averts each catastrophe in consultation with Enki, including undergoing an Enochian dream vision, and escapes the final destruction by building a boat.[11] The Ark in Genesis 6:14 is described as being covered with *kōper*, whose root is not found in Hebrew but is the Akkadian *kupru* (bitumen). This is a *hapax legomenon*, being the singular occurrence of the word in the Old Testament, and thus must be considered a vestigial remain from the earlier textual tradition, as there is a perfectly serviceable Hebrew equivalent. It is a final proof, making it impossible to deny that Genesis is based on Mesopotamian texts. *Atra-Hasis* provides the antecedent for the mythologies of Enoch and Noah, and thence of Prometheus and Deucalion in the Greek telling of the same tale. Prometheus on his crag becomes, in due course, one of the most romantic 'pagan' images of Lucifer, suffering and torn for his altruistic theft of divine knowledge.

Atrahasis sacrifices in thanks for being delivered into safety, and the famished gods cluster about the sacrifice 'like flies.'[12] This is paralleled in Genesis 8:20-21:

And Noah builded an altar unto the Lord; and took of every clean beast, and of every clean fowl, and offered burnt offerings on the altar. And the Lord smelled a sweet savour; and the Lord said in his heart, I will not again curse the ground any more for man's sake; for the imagination of man's heart is evil from his youth; neither will I again smite any more every thing living, as I have done.

After the deluge, the gods regulate the population by means of sterility, stillbirth, infant mortality and the office of the chaste priestess.[13] Whilst this appears to give credence to the over-population thesis, we cannot cleave this from the blood song of rebellion. Silvia Federici's reading of the early modern witch hunts shows that social and sexual control are intrinsically linked.[14] I suggest there is a similar authoritarian dynamic at work here. Like Genesis, *Atra-Hasis* is a discourse on the limits of human powers, and the establishment of a covenant. Yet for oath breakers, it provides a vista of our divine inheritance, should we wish to oppose the tyranny of kings. It falls upon some generations to renew the war, and thus the pact.

A Mass of Blood and Feathers

The books of Enoch are to be approached with some trepidation; and
it is not because they are in some way repressed texts that struck
terror into the Church for containing secret knowledge. The reasons
for their exclusion, I will deal with in due course. Extracts from
them, notably the work of early ninth century Byzantine monk
Syncellus, meant that the material was available, even when officially
redacted from the canon. Milton – that great unwitting patron of
the romantic Satan – had, through this source, the bulk of 1 Enoch
6–10 to draw upon for his portraiture. This comprises the most
important material, encapsulating the entire fallen angels tradition.[1]
It has never been truly absent.

The books of Enoch smoke like mountain peaks promising a
pure white land of angelic majesty, of forbidden wisdom borne by
the messengers of the stars. John Dee and his Enochian project[2] are
testament to the esteem in which these missing books were held,
a corpus of unknown extent, a dream that would lead to a golden
age, a schematic catalogue of the akashic library whose stacks were
ghosted with allegory. Yet to understand the older works, not those
dictated by ambiguous intercessors, requires going to the opposite
extreme, to set them firmly on the ground and reveal the heavenly
garments mired in blood. These are the texts of a people ensanguined

in strife. Without this context the monstrous actions of the giants and the import of the Enochic books remains flittingly elusive.

The dating of the books of Enoch was once contentious; and the argument proposed that they predated Genesis. If this was the case, they would represent the ur-wisdom, the text that orthodoxy over-wrote. For alternative historians, as well as witchcraft practitioners seeking an origin myth, this was very seductive. But the proposal has been tempered. In fact, the very opening line of 1 Enoch relies on Genesis, and the contentious Genesis 6:1–4 that I have studied so closely is required for 1 Enoch 6–11. The books of Enoch are clearly post-exilic and bring in Canaanite, Hittite, Phoenician and Greek sources. These are highly complex documents; 1 Enoch, though reli-ant on Genesis, is in turn fed into by the mighty rivers of *Atra-Hasis* and the Mesopotamian sapiential traditions, making its origins ulti-mately impossible to date. However, 1 Enoch can be contextualised, and indeed must be, whilst not neglecting the spring from which it babbled forth.

Rowley and Bartelmus propose that Enoch chronicles the op-pression under Antiochus IV (Antiochus Epiphanes), c.215–164 BCE, as given in the apocryphal Maccabees and described by Josephus in his *Antiquities of the Jews*. Antiochus is the 'little horn,' the proto-antichrist figure in Daniel 8.[3] Antiochus is depicted in these texts as suppressing a rebellious people, but historians now see him, more realistically, as intervening in a civil war between the Orthodox Jews of the countryside and the Hellenised Jews of Jerusalem. Antiochus is an attractive match: he is the mad king who bans burnt offerings, the Sabbath and circumcision, whilst restoring idolatry and sacri-ficing swine flesh. He goes so far as to set up the 'abomination of desolation,' a statue of Zeus in the now defiled Second Temple.[4] But the rule of Antiochus is not the only backdrop to consider.

Nickelsburg and Kvanvig are two prominent scholars who dis-agree, dating 1 Enoch to the Diadochan wars of 323 to 302 BCE, as the successors of Alexander the Great fought over Palestine. The country changed hands seven times in an era of carnage and dislocation. The history is briefly related in the introductory passages of 1 Maccabees, and is prior to the accession of Antiochus:

> And after his death [Alexander] they all put crowns upon themselves; so did their sons after them many years: and evils were multiplied in the earth.

A 21 year period of hated governments, ceaseless warfare, acquisitive taxation, expropriation and on-going Hellenisation provoked a religious response. The context of the Diadochan wars lays bare 1 Enoch as an attack upon the idea of the divinity of kingship; a claim which was used by the Hellenistic rulers to buttress their legitimacy. Whoever scrabbled to the top of the bloody heap wanted to present their rule as a continuation of Alexander's god-given Imperium. In 1 Enoch the war is still raging, which is perhaps the strongest evidence we have to date it: the end of the fourth century. It is almost impossible to imagine the sense of disorder wrought by the collapse of empire, except when viewed through the apocalyptic texts that it spawns; 1 Enoch is such a text. The scant lines in Maccabees might be passed over, but the cannibalistic giants of 1 Enoch impress themselves on the historical record and demand analysis.

My preference is to side with this timing, but my argument does not rely upon it. Either way, whether the Diadochan wars or the reign of Antiochus, the Enochic texts are the children of war and disorder, whose clear propagandist aims were often concealed within the language of apocalypticism. Its polyvalence is part of the reason that such works have had enduring appeal. The apocalyptic discourse granted an escape from the chaos of the present into a mythic narrative that led to an eschatological salvation. This explains how apocalypticism has been able to persist, penetrating through cultural and temporal membranes with ease. New faces are cast into old roles, and current events read allegorically.

Having stated this, as a necessary redress to the common misconceptions about 1 Enoch, the fact remains that it does contain significantly older traditions than Genesis 6:1–4. The very brevity of that passage does more than imply a parallel or preceding textual or oral lore: it confirms it. 1 Enoch is the heir to these strands, although it would be unwise to then assume that it is an immaculate transmission. The evidence postulates the existence of an ur-text, in Aramaic, and possibly even Hebrew, which remains lost to history. The Book of Noah, first posited by Charles, is now taken as a solid fact; fragments of a Noah apocalypse in Hebrew have been discovered, and it seems such a tradition was drawn upon by the composer of 1 Enoch. My interest is not in seeking to reconstruct this text, but in the trajectory of the narrative. For the sake of accuracy it is necessary to observe that the oldest material in 1 Enoch sits alongside interjections and sections added centuries later. John Joseph Collins[5] shows the complexity inherent in the material under examination:

> The opening chapter of 1 Enoch is a patchwork of biblical phrases, alluding *inter alia* to Balaam's oracle in Numbers 23–24. This allusiveness enriches the language by building associations and analogies between the biblical contexts and the new context in which the phrase is used. It also means that this language lends itself to different levels of meaning and becomes harder to pin down in a univocal, unambiguous way.

This is more helpful than Gunkel's verdict that it is a 'disorderly mess of traditions'; or what Beer calls 'chaotic swirled together material'; or the sheer exasperation of Goudge's 'this stupid book.' Such judgements reflect the desire for order, but do not help us to comprehend the text. The quote from Collins bears re-reading. It gives an understanding of the way in which what I have come to think of as the 'apocalyptic machine' generates scripture, which in turn is critical in unlocking the meaning behind Lucifer. He is the result of the same processes whose genealogy I am tracing, as much as he is an amalgam of historical figures, whether mythic or historic. The enduring archaic meaning is tailored to the needs of the present and thus undergoes periodic revision. This confirms that there cannot be an appeal to a state of original purity; Lucifer is constantly immanent, a heavy static that illuminates now and now, and then now, as lightning does. What can be elucidated is the allusions, associations and analogies that recur throughout the texts, and thus comprise a tradition. This is why there is a need to be saturated with scripture, with Apocrypha, with the languages and koiné of the ancient past, as a poet must continually baptise themself in the river of languages and literatures that irrigate our culture. One cannot limit Lucifer to a moment, or extract him from the river of history that runs as surely as Eridanus flows.

It is not the aim of this chapter to give a complete breakdown of the Enochic tradition, which would be implausible. Here I shall look at those aspects of the tradition that have informed our idea of Lucifer. The best source for academic Enoch scholars is now the edition of Black and VanderKam, which supersedes the previous work of Robert Henry Charles. Though Charles remains heavily cited, due in part to his use of language which has the mellifluous quality of the KJV, it has significant shortcomings.

The Charles edition of 1906 is based on the 1821 first edition of Laurence, who rescued the texts, brought back from Ethiopia by explorer James Bruce in 1773, that were mouldering, neglected in the stacks. This provided the Western world with a book that had been known about in Europe since the end of the fifteenth century; though it is not a text that was unseen, as I have noted, Syncellus had been available since the 1606 edition of J.J. Scaliger's *Thesaurus temporem*.[6]

Charles relied on the only available sources at the time, the Ge'ez Ethopian texts supplemented with the Greek. Further evidence was drawn from the discovery of another Greek version (eighth century CE) of 1 Enoch in the desert necropolis of Akhmim in Egypt, carefully placed in the grave of a Christian monk with other apocalyptic manuscripts.

The work of Charles predated the significant modern discovery of the Aramaic fragments in Qumran. These leather scrolls found in cave 4, are truly fragments, a confetti of letters, often only clarifying a single sign.[7] But it is these fragments which have provided the most accurate names for the fallen angels through the most painstaking work imaginable. These texts had fallen out of favour in the Qumran community by the first century CE. Some were being re-used, for example in schoolboy's exercises, making the discoveries of Milik a veritable miracle. The early Christian community, that became frenetically obsessed with the Enochic literature, did not have this source, relying instead on the Greek version. Ours is therefore the first generation of practitioners of magic and witchcraft who are able to again vocalise, however hesitantly, the earliest attested names for the fallen angels.

Intense comparative work on the Ethiopian and Greek variants has provided the bulk of the changes that make up the Black and VanderKam version, which, though attempting to keep the cadence of the Charles, is an academic rather than a poetic rendering. For magical use, it is to this I have turned, as the spirit names are mis-spelled or missing in the Charles. I have tabulated the most recent work on these names from Black and VanderKam, with the Aramaic spelling and gematria value for those so inclined in the Appendix. In keeping with their presentation of the work, [square brackets] denote a parenthesis from the Greek text. This restoration presents a spirit list that predates the most commonly considered ancestor of the grimoires, the *Testament of Solomon*.[8] The celestial, divinatory and metallurgical skills of the Enochic angels has significant parallels with the grimoire tradition; the *Lemegeton* in particular, which places itself within the fallen angel tradition, albeit influenced by *Picatrix* and decanate/mansion imagery.

1 Enoch is not a grimoire as such, it is an apocalyptic eschatology that must be inverted if it is to be used *contra christ*. It was never intended to summon, but rather to reassure that a binding could be accomplished and a final victory won.

The most important text to consider in regard to Lucifer is The Book of Watchers, first titled as such by Syncellus in the ninth century, and that, from the surviving Ethiopic source, is designated 1 Enoch 1–36. As one would expect, from the comments of the academics, even this brief section can be subdivided into different authors and myths. Our focus is made yet more precise: the verses 6–11, a discrete unit in this turbulent text, which tells the story of the rebellion in heaven, expanding upon the tantalising mythology we have encountered in Genesis 6.

The importance of Enoch for the Lucifer mythos is that it shifts the point of gravity in Genesis to the rebellion of the divine and semidivine beings, the giants. The concept of evil was previously attached to the state of primeval disorder (Genesis 1–4), and subsequently man (Adam). By privileging the rebellion, a new etiology for the origin of evil was proposed, one which gained dominance in a Judaism at war, and went on to inform, not only the nascent Jesus movement and gnostic speculation, but the Church fathers and Christianity into the early medieval period.[9] Evil was given independent existence as a race of beings; a theological move into the dangerous territory of dualism. Central to this endeavour was the emergence of the figure of Lucifer, who rose from the undifferentiated primordial chaos of Genesis and passed through the matrix of the angelic teachers and memories of the Mighty Dead to become something entirely new. Evil was being personified, and its origin accounted for.

Paradoxically, this emergent dualism would eventually be used to counter gnostic heresies. The Church Fathers sought to supplant the dualism proposed by the Gnostics (and, in some sense, by Marcion) of the Old Testament God as demiurge and Christ/Serpent as redeemer. They could only acheive this by drawing the enemy figure more boldly in their exegesis of the Old Testament. This meant forging the serpent of Eden, the Watchers and the combat myth into a narrative structure that would merge seamlessly into New Testament concerns with exorcism and the demonology of Paul. Again, Paul can only be understood in reference to the rival traditions he was polemicising against.[10] Essentially, an enemy was required to make God good. The fallen angel story was used for this purpose, combatting the persistent dualist heresy that Christianity has coiled around its heart. I will return to this in more detail later in the text.

I will now précis 1 Enoch 6–11 before examining it in detail. The

Watcher angels rebel and descend, taking human women as wives who give birth to a race of giants. The Watchers impart teachings, notably astrology, weaponry, root-cutting, spells and cosmetics. A slaughter ensues as the giants rampage. Those unjustly murdered at the hands of the giant offspring of the Watchers petition God, whose archangels imprison the rebellious watchers under the earth. The giants are then killed by the flood unleashed by God. It is a very different text to the bone naked account of Genesis 6:1–4.

It is useful to reproduce the text of 1 Enoch 6–11, which has the benefit of allowing the original voices to speak, and upon which I will then make my own observations.

> And it came to pass, when the children of men had multiplied, in those days were born unto them beautiful and comely daughters. And watchers, children of heaven, saw them and desired them and lusted after them; and they said one to another: 'Come, let us choose for ourselves wives from among the daughters of earth and let us beget us children.' And Semhazah, who was their leader, said unto them: 'I fear ye will not want to do this deed, and I alone shall pay the penalty for a great sin.' And they all answered him and said: 'Let us all swear an oath, that we shall not depart, any of us from this plan until we carry it out and do this deed.' Then they all swore together and bound one another with imprecations. And they were two hundred; who descended in the days of Jared on the summit of Mount Hermon; and they called the mount Hermon, because they swore and bound one another with imprecations upon it. And these are the names of their leaders: Šemhazah, their chief; Arteqif, second to him; Ramtel, third to him; Kokabel, fourth to him; Urel, fifth to him; Ramel, sixth to him; Danel, seventh to him; Ziqel, eighth to him; Baraqel, ninth to him; Asael, tenth to him; Hermoni, eleventh to him; Matrel, twelfth to him; Ananel, thirteenth to him; Sithwael, fourteenth to him; Simsel, fifteenth to him; Sahrel, sixteenth to him; Tammel, seventeenth to him; Turel, eighteenth to him; Yammel, nineteenth to him; Zehorel, twentieth to him. These are the leaders and their dekadarchs.

We begin with a very clear paraphrasing of Genesis 6:1–4, with an angelic descent engendered by lust. The angels, and not the beautiful and comely daughters, are to blame. This is, I stress, not a fall but a rebellion, made concrete through a pact. The mutual swearing is a feature of later demonology, as is the intimation of a hidden conspiracy – which is how witchcraft comes to be characterised. The translation, however, does not convey the weight of this pact. It is a vow sworn on the condition of total destruction: a swearing on one's life, in the Hebrew חרם (herem). A sense of this is provided in the black fast accounted in Acts 23:14, 'And they came to the chief priests and elders, and said, We have bound ourselves under a great curse, that we will eat nothing until we have slain Paul.' It remains a staple technique of witchcraft, of the hungry and the poor.

Ironically, the term 'watchers,' the name for these angels in the Greek translation, comes from the functionaries of the Assyrian security state; they are literally 'the eyes of the king.' The descent is, like the Genesis account, given a time, the days of Jared, but crucially it is also given a location, Mount Hermon or Harmon.[11] The highest point in the Levant, Harmon is a triple limestone peak rising 1800 metres above sea level; it is the equivalent of the Mount Zaphon of Isaiah, indeed the two are often conflated. Both are described as Northern mountains, swathed in darkness. Now the stories of Azazel, Hêlēl Ben Šaḥar and the watchers coalesce, the storm circling around a specific mythic locus whose competing peaks, whilst geographically distinct, have a unity of meaning as *axis mundi*.

Having clarified the topography of our myth we can take in the kite's view and soar over the whole Transjordan. What we see is not the biblical terrain that we might expect, but a megalithic landscape strewn with hundreds of ancient monuments. According to the archaeological survey of Karge,[12] the Israelites regarded these dolmens as the tombs of the mighty Rephaim; which seems inevitable due to the cyclopean dimensions of the structures. The 'bed of Og' is one such site and described in Deuteronomy 3:11:

For only Og king of Bashan remained of the remnant of giants;

behold, his bedstead was a bedstead of iron; is it not in Rabbath of the children of Ammon? nine cubits was the length thereof, and four cubits the breadth of it, after the cubit of a man.

No doubt, 'iron' is used here because of its figurative association with strength, harshnesh and oppression. The actual structure is basalt. Clearly, only giants could have made such edifices. The passage from Deuteronomy suggests a dolmen.[13] In his comprehensive study, Karge communicates some of the awe the dolmens inspire:

> The large specimens ... make a massive, primeval impression. The high set, usually quite raw, unworked plates which form the Dolmen and perched above them the massive capstones, are exquisitely adapted to the character of the land and show the megalithic thinking, it is monumental purity personified. Working it would have desecrated the stone and detracted from its impact.

The dolmens became centres of hero cults. The dolmens appeared from 5000 BCE in the Transjordan, predominantly in the mountain region from Hebron to Galilee. As there are no carvings on them, all we can attest is that the people who made them laid great stress on burial, as the dolmens are unmistakeably tombs, and the offerings discovered have been simple shells. This makes dating contentious; though it is possible that they date to the pre-pottery Neolithic – which is the date of the earliest European dolmens – other comparable sites, such as those in the Caucasus, date from the advanced Bronze Age. Regardless of the difficulty of dating, this physical evidence explains the Old Testament view that the Rephaim are the prehistoric inhabitants of Canaan, which became associated with the later cult of the Mighty Dead. The bare walls lead us to contemplate the mystery of our lost human origins. Our angels have dwelling places.[14]

The angels are enumerated and given names. The Black and VanderKam version differs here significantly from Clark, who omits the full twenty, and has markedly different orthography. Each leader is a dekadarch, which indicates that he has ten subordinates beneath him, giving us the total of 200 Watchers.[15]

The rubric about the number of angels beneath the chiefs is a staple in later grimoires, such as the previously cited *Lemegeton*. The grimoires are often seen as a late phenomenon, a pastiche, when on the contrary, they demonstrate the continuity of a tradition in the West built on Near Eastern principles that stretch back to Sumeria at the very least.

In 1 Enoch 6 a new character is introduced: Šemhazah. A leader of the Angels, whose name seems to be a combination of *šem* (the name) and *azaza* (rebellion).[16] Šemhazah, the leader of the 200 angels, is called Samlazaz in other translations. There are, in fact, many variant spellings of this angelic name, which might suggest an oral tradition, most likely in the Midrash, the interpretation of scripture provided by Rabbis following readings of the Torah. But it additionally reflects the different languages in use: Ge'ez, Hebrew, Aramaic and Greek, as well as a non-standardised orthography. Furthermore, it is suggested by VanderKam and Black that the spirit list is a legacy from an older source, or sources.[17] The angels have names, but they are weathered like gravestones. The version I have provided is the most accurate available to date, and even this is marked by omissions and conjecture. Continuing to 1 Enoch 7 we garner more details.

These (leaders) and all the rest (of the two hundred watchers) took for themselves wives, from all whom they chose; and they began to cohabit with them and to defile themselves with them, and they taught them sorcery and spells, and showed them the cutting of roots and herbs. And they became pregnant by them, and bore great giants, of three thousand cubits; and there were [not] born upon earth offspring [which grew to their strength]. They devoured the entire fruits of men's labour, and men were unable to sustain them. Then the giants treated them violently and began to slay mankind. They began to do violence to and to attack all the birds, and beasts, and reptiles [that crawl upon the earth], and the fish of the sea, and they began to devour their flesh, and they were drinking the blood. Thereupon the earth made accusation against the lawless ones.

This chapter continues to expound upon the interbreeding of women and angels in Genesis 6:4. The square brackets denote the Greek source, which suggests that no other children were born, thus explaining the rise of the giants. It then introduces a new element, that of teaching, a motif that is entirely absent in the first book of the Bible and the other sources for Lucifer we have examined thus far. Witchcraft is predicated on the myth of instruction by fallen angels, of whom Lucifer is the presumed chief, which is a fusion of 1 Enoch with the fallen king of Isaiah. Now, having obtained a greater understanding of the meaning and origin of ancient kingship, one can appreciate how the two strands have been congruently drawn together. The king was an inheritor and living repository of the ancient wisdom of his ancestors, and the temple complex (particularly in Mesopotamia) was the home of all the craft skills. Witchcraft is the progeny of this conjunction, having divine ancestral lineage and an operative techne.

The arts enumerated here (sorcery, spells, root and herb cutting), are those of folk magic and witchcraft. In 1 Enoch it is explicitly women who receive the transmission. Male-centric versions of modern witchcraft fail to highlight this important aspect of the story, preferring instead to gloss that the fallen angels taught 'mankind.' One ritual approach is to use *Serpent–Eve–Adam* as the pattern for male initiation, and *Angel–Daughters of Eve* as the pattern for female initiation.

Instruction by otherworldly teachers is characteristic of all magical cultures; in this instance we can suggest an origin: the Apkallu sages. These Sumerian wisdom figures are not commonly cited in witchcraft or magical traditions, due to their antiquity and the previous biases in (biblical) scholarship. The Apkallu were the seven sages who brought civilisation to men before the flood. The appearance of these beings as half fish/half men suggests a stellar aspect, as the glinting of fish in the waters was often compared to the movement of the stars in the heavens. Fish, and likewise snakes, are wisdom figures in shamanic cultures. It is entirely possible that the legend of the Apkallu informed the story of the rebel angels, as it was known in the period through the history of Babylon, the *Babyloniaca* of Berossus.[18] However, the fish godman Oannes is not an exact match for the leader of the rebel angels; he emerges from the sea rather than descending from a mountain. Yet these stories share an ambivalent relationship between the teaching deities and man. The sages are eventually expelled, for unspecified reasons; whereas the rebel angels create disorder and bloodshed, which leads to their banishment.[19] There is a deep uneasiness in our relationship with the city and the arts of civilisation that engender it, an angst that I Enoch is heir to. As I have shown in my discussion of the Deuter-onomists, it is the company of heaven to whom the opprobrium is attached in Judaism. I Enoch, whether it originated in polemics against Babylon, Canaan, Ugarit or the proto-Jewish religion, is the *caput mortuum* from which a witchcraft tradition has germinated.

Demonstrably, sex with otherworldly teaching spirits is a pan-cultural shamanic experience, from the serpent god who is lover to the *miko* of Japan[20] to Siberian shamanism[21] and, as I argue, the sabbat congress of devil and witch, who are our most congruent cultural archetypes. The teaching angels of the Enochic tradition were assimilated with indigenous European myths and encounter experiences. As the imperial religion of Christianity gained domi-nance over pagan and animistic beliefs, such problematic epiphanies would become scripted by the inquisitors. Native concepts of faery and familiar are where the origins of European witchcraft reside. The teaching encounter has a sexual component, and is given in particular, though not exclusively, to women. Many of the witch-craft myths that cite the fallen angels are therefore etiologies for the experience of direct teachings from divine beings.

Returning to our text, the excesses of the giants should be under-stood in the context of the composition of I Enoch, that is, the Diadochan wars. The giants here are the rival successors of Alexan-der warring over Palestine. The natural order, established in Genesis, is violated in a thinly disguised polemic. The drinking of blood harks back to the importance of blood in *Atra-Hasis* and has the additional sacrilegious import of violating the purity laws laid down in Leviticus. This is not vampirism, but an image of ceaseless warfare.

1 Enoch 8 continues with an extremely important chapter that fleshes out the kinds of teachings which are bestowed – what would be considered in grimoire terms, the statement of powers:

> And Asael taught men to make swords of iron and breastplates of bronze and every weapon for war; and he showed them the metals of the earth, how to make gold, to fashion [adornments] and about silver, to make bracelets for women; and he instructed them about antimony, and eye-shadow, and all manner of precious stones and dyes and varieties of adornments; and the children of men fashioned for themselves and for their daughters and transgressed; and there arose much impiety on the earth, and they committed fornication and went astray, and corrupted their ways. Semhazah taught spell-binding and the cutting of roots; Hermoni taught the loosing of spells, magic, sorcery and sophistry. Baraqel taught the auguries of the lightning, Kokabiel taught the auguries of the stars; Zikiel taught the auguries of fire-balls; Arteqif taught the auguries of earth, Simsel taught the auguries of the sun; Sahrel taught the auguries of the moon. And they began to reveal secrets to their wives. Then the giants began to devour the flesh of men, and mankind began to become few upon the earth; and as men perished from the earth, their voice went up to heaven: 'Bring our cause before the Most High, and our destruction before the glory of the Great One.'

The most vital of transgressions given is that of metallurgy. Its primacy here designates this as a text from a time of war. Asael (Azazel) is given as the patron of artificers and, by extension, alchemy. Strangely, it seems in this chapter that Asael/Azazel is predominant, with Šemhazah secondary. Again, students of the grimoires will be aware of the fluid, apparently arbitrary, way in which hierarchies come down to us. Clearly, 1 Enoch combines at least two traditions: one which told of Azazel and another that spoke of Šemhazah. The same process of combination is evinced in the evolution of Lucifer: the synthesis of allied figures into a single named entity whose dominance effaces what is a tortured genealogy.

Asael/Azazel can be linked to the Dactyls and Curetes, who were likewise earth-born giants, and figure prominently in Stratton-Kent's *Geosophia*.[22] They belong to a complex of magical metal workers from the iron-fingered mountains of Asia Minor. This directs our attention back to the archaic mysteries and their ritual pattern of death, descent to the underworld and rebirth amongst the company of gods. A mythic cycle that Christianity has sought to dominate, that shamanism embodied and that modern magic can reinstate.

Nickelsburg[23] makes the case for the figure of Prometheus as an origin for Azazel. In Aeschylus' *Prometheus Bound*, he boasts of his many skills, from observing the stars, to domesticating animals, to medicine and augury, finishing with this passage [500-505]:

> Now as to the benefits to men that lay concealed beneath the earth – bronze, iron, silver, and gold – who would claim to have discovered them before me? No one, I know full well, unless he likes to babble idly. Hear the sum of the whole matter in the compass of one brief word – every art possessed by man comes from Prometheus.

Metallurgy is coterminous with the fall of man. Metal allows the plough to furrow the earth and the axe to hew down the great cedars; it is the instrument and the motive for culture, civilisation and war. The author of 1 Enoch smelts in the great forge the sword of bloodshed and the gold and silver bangles that adorn the wives of the angels. The ground oxides and antimony beautify at the cost of men sent into the bowels of the earth. Those who work with these elements are inevitably to be shunned. Tubal Cain as first smith is tainted by this association.[24] The smith has always been a figure of taboo in culture, as has the executioner, butcher and sacrificial priest. In order to construct a rite that embodies these aspects of the tradition, iron and gold will have a central role in the mystery.

It is significant that the passage artfully blends the cosmetic arts and chemistry with those of warfare and metallurgy. The relationship of women and war is deep-rooted and complex; the goddess presides over the battlefield and the bedchamber, and the arts of love and war form the knot that fastens her girdle. The anathemising of adornment is found consistently in the Bible, notably in the story of Jezebel, as related in 2 Kings 9:30, in which she paints her face and gazes forth from her window, in the attitude of both the goddess and prostitute, and in the odious Jeremiah 4:30 which presages Revelation:

> And when thou art spoiled, what wilt thou do? Though thou clothest thyself with crimson, though thou deckest thee with ornaments of gold, though thou rentest thy face with painting, in vain shalt thou make thyself fair; thy lovers will despise thee, they will seek thy life.

Though the angels descend through their lust in 1 Enoch 6, 1 Enoch 8 makes a subtle change of inference; now it is woman who is deemed culpable. Woman, whose power is often equated with, if not confined to, her interiority, has magico-sexual power over the spirits – her binding is exercised through the spell of attraction, rather than coercion. It is a virtue that underpins the mutual identification of priestess, courtesan, actress and witch. Seduction is a proven method of spirit working.

In the inventory of arts, metallurgy is followed by the making of spells, the breaking of enchantments, rootcutting, sophistry and sorcery. All the subsequent skills enumerated are divinatory arts: astrology, knowledge of the constellations, nephomancy, geomancy, and the course of the sun and moon. These appear to be arranged in contrasting dyads making/breaking, lightning/stars, comets/earth, sun/moon. Augury is a pagan practice, and forbidden in Judaism. Witness Isaiah 47:13, where Babylon is upbraided and mocked, 'Let now the astrologers, the stargazers, the monthly prognosticators, stand up, and save thee from these things that shall come upon thee.' Babylon as the home of starry wisdom is the old enemy and its practices culturally taboo. Henryk Drawnel suggests that the skills listed in 1 Enoch are those of the *āšipu* – professional enchanters, healers and astronomers linked to the Babylonian Temple – and that this is a polemic against them.

1 Enoch 9 follows:

Then Michael, Sariel, Raphael, and Gabriel looked down from the sanctuary in heaven, and they saw much blood shed on the earth; and the whole earth was full of godlessness and violence which men were committing against it. [And they went in] and said to [the angels]: 'The voice and cry of the children of earth are ascending to the gates of heaven. Now to you, the holy ones of heaven, the souls of men are making their suit, complaining with groans and saying: 'Bring our case before the Most High, and our destruction before the glory of the Great One.' Then [Raphael] and Michael [and Sariel and Gabriel] went in and said to the Lord of the ages: 'Thou art our great Lord, Lord of the ages, Lord of lords and God of gods, and King of the ages; and thy glorious throne is for all generations of eternity, and thy Name is holy and great and praised unto all ages! For thou art he who has created all things, and hast power over all; and all things are revealed and unconcealed before you; and thou seest all things, and there is nothing can be hid from you. Thou seest what Asael has done, what he has introduced and taught, wrong-doing, and sins upon the earth, and all manner of guile in the land; that he revealed the eternal mysteries prepared in heaven and made them known to men, and his abominations the initiates among the children of men make for themselves. Šemhazah instructed men in spell-binding, (he) whom thou hast appointed ruler of all spell-binders. And they cohabited with the daughters of the men of the earth, and had intercourse with them, and they were defiled by the females, and revealed to them all manner of sins, and taught them to make hate-charms.

And now behold! the daughters of men brought forth from them sons, giants, bastards; and much blood was spilled upon the earth, and the whole earth was filled with wickedness. And now, behold! the souls of mortal men are crying and making their suit to the gates of heaven; and their groaning has ascended, and they cannot escape the wrongs that are being done on the earth. But thou knowest all things before they come to pass, and thou seest them and hast let them alone; and thou dost not say to us what we should do with regard to them on account of these things.'

This chapter requires only brief comment. The original order of Michael, Sariel, Raphiel and Gabriel is given.[25] The archangels are implored by the bloodshed wrought by the giants to petition Yahweh and are joined in this by the still wet souls of the dead. It is a lament for Israel torn by war. The voice and cry that reaches heaven is reminiscent of the clamour in *Atra-Hasis*, and here too it is a prelude to destruction by the flood.

The angels are said to be defiled by their congress with women. Such interspecies coition could be considered as sex magical ritual, whose purpose is to engender heroes. These men of renown are the result of such divine/human cross-matching, found in myths across the ancient world. It is notably true of the Greek and Canaanite heroes as well as Gilgameš, who was born of the union of Lugalbanda and Ninsun. The giants born to the daughters of men are flesh and blood, and the women are condemned for their actions. The acquiescence of women in provoking sin, and thereby allowing evil to flourish, is played out in persistent Christian antifeminism. By absolving God of creating evil angels, woman is made to shoulder the blame.

The endgame against the watchers and giants follows, in 1 Enoch 10, and due to the complexity and length of the passage it requires a concurrent exegesis rather than the pendant commentary I have employed up until this point:

Then the Most High said and the great Holy One spoke up and sent Sariel to the son of Lamech, saying: 'Go to Noah and say to him in my Name "Hide yourself!" and show him the End that is approaching: that the earth will be completely destroyed, and tell him that a Deluge is about to come on the whole earth, to destroy all things from the face of the earth. And now instruct the righteous one what to do, and the son of Lamech, that he may save his life and escape for all time; and from him a plant shall be planted and established for all generations forever.'

The reason given for the destruction of the world is not that of Genesis, the wickedness of man, but is entirely laid at the feet of the fallen angels, and the aperture opened up to them in the sin-craving bodies of women. Note that Sariel takes the role of intercessor (Enki in *Atra-Hasis*), whereas in Genesis, Noah speaks to God directly.

And to Raphael he said: 'Go, Raphael and bind Asael; fetter him hand and foot and cast him into darkness; make an opening in the desert, which is in the desert of Dudael, and there go and cast him in. And place upon him jagged and rough rocks, and cover him with darkness, and let him abide there for all time, and cover his face that he may not see light. And on the day of the great judgement he will be lead off to the blazing fire. Heal the earth which the watchers have ruined, and announce the healing of the earth, that I shall heal its wounds and that the children of men shall not altogether perish on account of the mysteries which the watchers have disclosed and taught the children of men. The whole earth has been devastated by the works of the teaching of Asael; record against him all sins.'

The judgement of the Lord is severe, but one can recognise the text it references, namely Leviticus. Yet in 1 Enoch, the scapegoat has become, not a sin offering, but a fully-fledged rival entity. He is specifically denied seeing the light, a critical aspect for rebirth as megalithic tomb alignments attest. The final burning, (the punishment alloted to witches), is not often commented upon. This represents a complete destruction as it dries up the marrow and the moisture of life required for resurrection. The fate of Asael is that of the red dragon of Revelation 12:7–9, who is cast into the earth:

> And there was war in heaven: Michael and his angels fought against the dragon; and the dragon fought and his angels, And prevailed not; neither was their place found any more in heaven. And the great dragon was cast out, that old serpent, called the Devil, and Satan, which deceiveth the whole world: he was cast out into the earth, and his angels were cast out with him.

This passage in Revelation would be inexplicable without recourse to the fallen angels tradition. 1 Enoch 10 then expands into an apocalyptic eschatology where a great judgement will occur with Asael cast into the fire. Ultimately, the same lot befalls the beast and the false prophet of Revelation 19:20:

> And the beast was taken, and with him the false prophet that wrought miracles before him, with which he deceived them that had received the mark of the beast, and them that worshipped his image. These both were cast alive into a lake of fire burning with brimstone.

Furthermore, Revelation 20:1–3 replicates the fettering of Asael in the temporal binding of dragon/Devil:

> And I saw an angel come down from heaven, having the key of the bottomless pit and a great chain in his hand. And he laid hold on the dragon, that old serpent, which is the Devil, and Satan, and bound him a thousand years, and cast him into the bottomless pit, and shut him up, and set a seal upon him, that he should deceive the nations no more, till the thousand years should be fulfilled: and after that he must be loosed a little season.

Revelation is heir to Enoch in that it transmits the story of the fall of the angels, a story only briefly alluded to in Genesis. Moreover,

Revelation has been a constant companion, even after the Enochic fallen angel tradition was excommunicated by the church. With one condensed sentence the Devil, Satan, the beast, the false prophet, the dragon and the old serpent are revealed as one being: the deceiver. So too, by extension, we can consider Asael/Azazel as belonging to this litany of masks. For those who seek to parse Lucifer from his full genealogy this is highly problematic.

The binding and confinement of the malefactor in 1 Enoch and Revelation is analogous with the crime and punishment of Prometheus, of which we read in Hesiod's *Theogony*:

> And ready-witted Prometheus he bound with inextricable bonds, cruel chains, and drove a shaft through his middle, and set on him a long-winged eagle, which used to eat his immortal liver; but by night the liver grew as much again everyway as the long-winged bird devoured in the whole day.

Prometheus is chastised for a similar breach to that of the Watchers: bringing fire from heaven and teaching man every art. A deliberate transgression against the order established by Zeus. He is notably a giant (Titan), another detail that demonstrates a familial mythic relationship. It is unlikely that Prometheus is the rock upon which Enoch is built however, but most likely represents a diffusion, as Astour suggests. When Enoch is excluded from the canon, the legend of Prometheus is drawn upon to create our portrait of Lucifer; a figure who becomes increasingly sympathetic, for, unlike the watchers, he is allowed to speak. Indeed, the entire Titanomachy follows the parabolic descent of the Watchers. A bronze anvil falling into the resounding chasm of gloomy Tartarus, and Zeus the sky god triumphing after a protracted war.

In 1 Enoch, the judgement continues:

> And to Gabriel the Lord said: 'Go Gabriel, to the giants, (their) bastard offspring, the children of fornication, and destroy (those) sons of the watchers from among the sons of men. Muster them

(for battle), and send them one against the other in a battle of destruction. Length of days shall not be theirs: they shall all request (it) of you, but no petition shall be granted to their fathers on their behalf, that they should not expect to live an eternal life, but that each one of them should live five hundred years.'

The incessant conflict of the Diadochan wars is the backdrop for the etiology of the bounding of life, as previously given in Genesis, and before that in *Gilgameš*.

And the Lord said to Michael: 'Go, make it known to Semhazah and the others who, with him, were united with the daughters of men, to defile themselves with them in their uncleanness. And when their sons shall be slain, and they see the destruction of their beloved ones, bind them for seventy generations in valleys of the earth, till the day of their judgement and of their consummation, until the great day of their judgement and the time of the end, until the judgement which is forever and ever becomes absolute. Then they shall be dragged off to the fiery abyss in torment, and in a place of incarceration they shall be imprisoned for all time.'

The fate of Šemhazah and his cohorts is paraphrased in the canonical 1 Jude 6–13 which relies on 1 Enoch,[26] opening thus, 'And the angels which kept not their first estate, but left their own habitation, he hath reserved in everlasting chains under darkness unto the judgement of the great day; and memorably concludes, 'wandering stars, to whom is reserved the blackness of darkness for ever.' The image is somewhat mistaken, as the wandering stars – a symbol of apostasy – are the planets, rather than the fallen watchers.[27] Nevertheless, Jude is another example of how elements of the Enochic tradition persisted in the canon and influenced Christian eschatology.

The angelic sin recounted here is explicitly sexual, highlighting the difficulty of 1 Enoch, which never seems sure whether the teaching of forbidden knowledge, or sex, is the root cause of evil. Perhaps the most graceful answer to this is that knowledge, in the biblical sense, contains both elements. Sophistry aside, what we actually have are two traditional accounts for the existence of evil: one which excuses God from culpability for creating evil by ascribing it to the rebel angels and women; the other polemicising against the astral deities and wisdom teachers of Babylonian and Canaanite origins.

> And everyone who is consumed by lust and is corrupted, from now on will be bound together with them and at the (fixed time) [of the judgement which] I shall judge, they shall perish for all generations forever. I shall destroy all the spirits of the bastard offspring of the watchers, because they wrong mankind. I shall destroy all iniquity from upon the face of the earth, and every evil work shall come to an end; and there shall appear the plant of righteousness; and it shall be a blessing, and deeds of righteousness shall be planted with joy for ever.

The plant of righteousness refers to the offspring of Noah, the righteous one.[28] But, given the need to curtail the lifespan of the giants and to explain human mortality, the image of the plant also evokes both the quest of Etana for the plant of birth and that of Gilgameš for the plant of youth.

There is one troubling inclusion in this passage – line 15 states 'I shall destroy all the spirits of the bastard offspring of the watchers, because they wrong mankind.' The promised destruction of the giants, which had seemed absolute, has gained a new aspect: the survival of their disembodied spirits. The narrative is extended to account for the persistent existence of illegitimate and evil entities. The idea is developed in 1 Enoch 15:8–12, which must be quoted, despite lying outside the core verses under consideration: (italics mine)

> And now the giants, who have produced from spirits and flesh, shall be called mighty spirits upon the earth, and on the earth shall be their dwelling place. *Evil spirits shall come forth from their bodies, for from men they have come, and from the holy watchers is the*

beginning of their creation and 'the beginning' of their origins. Evil spirits they shall be called upon the earth. As for celestial spirits, heaven shall be their dwelling-place: but for terrestrial spirits, born upon the earth, on the earth shall be their dwelling place. But the vicious spirits (issuing) from the giants, the Nephilim – they inflict harm, they destroy, they attack, they wrestle and dash to the ground, causing injuries; they eat nothing, but fast and thirst and produce hallucinations, and they collapse. And these spirits will rise against the sons of men and women, from whom they came forth.

This is the origin story of the spirits that the grimoires inherit, that of terrestrial and evil spirits whom it is considered legitimate to bind into service. They are the disincarnate spirits of the slaughtered giants, whose genealogy is a fusion of mortal woman and holy watcher. The Christian legality of such traffic with spirits is brokered by the guarantee of their final despatch to the fire as conveyed in Matthew 25:41, 'Then shall he say also unto them on the left hand, Depart from me, ye cursed, into everlasting fire, prepared for the devil and his angels.' They are the raw material of Western demonology. The demonologists positioned themselves to exploit a liminal space between the release of the spirits, required by eschatology, and their final destruction. Further variants on the fate of these spirits will be given in the following chapter, 'Children of Enoch'; of particular interest in this regard are the *Clementine Homilies*.

To conclude, any search for original purity in 1 Enoch is ultimately futile. The angels we seek are the gods, heroes, asterisms and celestial weather of pre-monotheist Judaism and its overlapping and rival cultures; they are not mere 'divels.' Lucifer as rebel has two precursors in Asael/Azazel and Šemhazah. The account given is not the thwarted ascent of spirit, but its reflex: the descent of spirit into matter. It is a particularly gnostic concern, which, in combination with Isaiah, enables us to close the ritual circle.

1 Enoch reworks the themes of *Atra-Hasis* and *Gilgameš*, whilst both pre- and post-dating Genesis. It turns the Diadochan wars into

a novel of apocalyptic magical realism. As a broad tradition it goes on to inform the New Testament and, in particular, Revelation. It contains the seed idea of witchcraft and shamanism, that of spirit encounter and initiation. 1 Enoch provides the earliest exemplar of the spirit catalogues of the grimoire tradition, though it is told from the side of its enemies, rather than laid out as a manual for practice in the manner of the *Testament of Solomon*. To innovate such an inversion is entirely permissible. In this chapter and the appendix, in which the spirit names are given and analysed, I have provided enough material for the practitioner to accomplish this end.

Children of Enoch

1 Enoch does not stand as a text in isolation, hence it would be remiss not to include other versions of the story, which I have styled as 'children of Enoch.' The texts I will consider are the apocryphal Jubilees, The Testament of the Twelve Patriarchs and the *Clementine Homilies*. It is by no means an exhaustive list of progeny, but these are both the most illustrative for my purpose, and the most influential. I will furthermore include the fallen angels material from the first century CE text of 2 Enoch,[1] 3 Enoch and the *Apocalypse of Abraham*. In conclusion the witch hunting manuals are cited for evidence that the fallen angel tradition is where the origin of witchcraft was sought.

From intertextual evidence, it is apparent that Jubilees is based on 1 Enoch and Genesis, with an origin in Jewish oral law. The work is generally dated between 170 and 150 BCE.[2] As a text, Jubilees did not garner widespread support in Judaism, but was preserved in Christian circles and became canonical in the Ethiopian and Abyssinian churches. First written in Hebrew, it was translated into Greek, then Latin, before being rendered into Ge'ez; the Ethiopic being the only surviving version of the complete text. Copies reached Europe with an edition by Dillman in 1859. R. H. Charles, the translator of 1 Enoch, produced what became the standard version in 1895, though it must be noted, his version was based on Dillman, not the manuscripts themselves. As with 1 Enoch, Charles took poetic and intuitive liberties with the text, and the modern academic approach to translation has markedly changed. Again, as with 1 Enoch, new Ethiopian versions have now come to light, in this case an additional 23 copies; so too have citations in Syriac and in the Dead Sea Scrolls.

Jubilees was, like 1 Enoch, not an entirely lost book, being known from references in Syncellus, Cedrenus and Epiphanius. It is of interest to us in that it preserves variants of the fallen angel mythos.

The writer of Jubilees is no longer thought of as a Pharisee, the position of R. H. Charles. Arguments as to his sect do not overtly concern this study, neither need I dwell on his schema for calendrical reform; my focus is explicitly on his demonology. Jubilees is essentially a rewritten text comprising Genesis and Exodus, often using direct quotes from these sources, which makes it particularly valuable for scholars seeking to understand the form of these base texts in the second century BCE. In the account of creation it gives three classes of angels: the angels of the presence, the angels of sanctification and a further order concerned with natural phenomena. The final class of angels in Jubilees 2:2 mirror those of 1 Enoch being the powers of fire, winds, clouds, darkness, snow, hail, frost, thunder and lightning. Jubilees is therefore shown to be reliant on 1 Enoch, though not slavishly so.

Against the angels are ranged demons, ruled by the prince of Mastêmâ, whose name means 'enmity,' and is cognate with Satan. Mention is further made of Beliar,[3] the leader of the Sons of Darkness in the theology of the Qumran community.

The legend of the fall as related in Jubilees admits key differences with the account of 1 Enoch. The angels descend, not driven by lust, but with divine sanction. Jubilees 4:15 reads:

the angels of the Lord descended on the earth, those who are named the Watchers, that they should instruct the children of men, and that they should do judgment and uprightness on the earth.

The teaching they give is notably regarded as positive, the writer of Jubilees is not engaging in a polemic against wisdom teachers. However, there is a class of illicit knowledge that Jubilees 8:3 warns against: Mesopotamian star lore. The text describes how Cainan,[4] son of Arp'ak'sad, finds:

> a writing which former (generations) had carved on the rock, and he read what was thereon, and he transcribed it and sinned owing to it; for it contained the teaching of the Watchers in accordance with which they used to observe the omens of the sun and moon and stars in all the signs of heaven.

One can conjecture that this rock was a boundary marker incised with the stellar heraldry of the Mesopotamian gods. A poetic image of a liminal encounter at the edge of what was considered to be the proper bounds of knowledge. Cainan is literally standing between cultures, the same relationship that the witch has between the human and otherworld as a hedge sitter.

The account of Jubilees does not blame the angels for actively teaching forbidden knowledge and therefore causing the flood. Their sin is suggested to be entirely sexual. The angels, like Adam and Eve, are not so much evil as weak, and this is the root of their disobedience. Jubilees is primarily concerned with intermarriage and purity, which at the time meant marrying your cousins, rather than the exogamy that the angel's union with the daughters of men represented. The passage quoted above ends with Cainan taking a wife outside of the house of Shem, which is precisely the transgression Jubilees cautions against.[5]

Jubilees 10: 5–12 concludes by making the offspring of the Watchers demons, as in 1 Enoch 15:8, and by naming their leader:

> And Thou knowest how Thy Watchers, the fathers of these spirits, acted in my day: and as for these spirits which are living, imprison them and hold them fast in the place of condemnation, and let them not bring destruction on the sons of thy servant, my God;

for these are malignant, and created in order to destroy. And let them not rule over the spirits of the living; for Thou alone canst exercise dominion over them. And let them not have power over the sons of the righteous from henceforth and for evermore. And the Lord our God bade us to bind all. And the chief of the spirits, Mastêmâ, came and said: 'Lord, Creator, let some of them remain before me, and let them harken to my voice, and do all that I shall say unto them; for if some of them are not left to me, I shall not be able to execute the power of my will on the sons of men; for these are for corruption and leading astray before my judgment, for great is the wickedness of the sons of men.' And He said: 'Let the tenth part of them remain before him, and let nine parts descend into the place of condemnation.' And one of us He commanded that we should teach Noah all their medicines; for He knew that they would not walk in uprightness, nor strive in righteousness. And we did according to all His words: all the malignant evil ones we bound in the place of condemnation and a tenth part of them we left that they might be subject before Satan on the earth. And we explained to Noah all the medicines of their diseases, together with their seductions, how he might heal them with herbs of the earth.

Mastêmâ takes the role of Satan in Job, as a functionary of God, not a rival to his power: obviously a different tradition to that of the Lucifer of Isaiah 14:12, though drawn from similar sources. For the author of Jubilees, the evil angels are an intrinsic component of the divine plan. Accordingly, the injustices that befall good men (for there are few good women in the Bible) are sanctioned by heaven. The demons are tithed, with one tenth left to roam the earth subject to the rule of Mastêmâ, and the rest of the bushels set aside in the apocalyptic storehouse. In Jubilees the burden of God's homicidal acts are placed upon Mastêmâ. He has the responsibility for bidding Abraham sacrifice Isaac, trying to murder Moses and hardening Pharaoh's heart against the fleeing Israelites, all acts previously credited to Yahweh. The binding of the evil spirits is identical to 1 Enoch, as is their origin, though they are ruled over by Mastêmâ in Jubilees, rather than Asael/Šemhazah.

At the end of the passage demons are identified as disease bringers with magico-medical remedies to thwart them – a trope of Sumerian, Egyptian and Greek magic, and the tale of Asmoday as given in Tobit and the *Testament of Solomon*. The cures are written in a book which is given to Shem (alternatively, Cham), son of Noah, who is an important figure in medieval magic. The magic book of Shem is a grimoire of exorcistic healing, one sanctioned by God.

Absent in Jubilees are the themes of rise, fall, forbidden teaching of women and kingship. Here there is no trace of Hanson's 'rebellion in heaven' motif. Equally, because the fall of Adam predates their descent, the Watchers are not culpable for sin nor identified with the serpent in the garden of Eden.[6] Jubilees merits inclusion precisely because the idea of the Satan begins to be delineated in this hybrid text. Here, as 'chief of (evil) spirits,' Mastêmâ can be considered the ruler of the netherworld, the inverse chthonic hierarchy of the demonised Rephaim. The shift that makes him the ultimate enemy of Yahweh, locked in an apocalyptic struggle, is yet to be implemented. At this juncture he is a sullen functionary testing the resolve of the faithful.

Jubilees is the record of a tradition in flux, with angels who seem more human than the lofty figures in I Enoch – closer to errant priests than deified wisdom teachers. The higher order of angels are even described as circumcised. Humans are responsible for their own sins, stimulated by an agent provocateur who acts within the schema of a just God. Those who do not partake of the covenant, i.e. all gentiles and apostates, are the 'children of destruction.'[7] This is the orthodox position, and also that of the Essene community and Qumran, where Jubilees was a popular text.

2 Enoch, the so called Slavonic Enoch, or Secrets of Enoch, is a late first century CE text. It is a blend of apocalyptic and mystical (early Merkabah) currents and distinct from the earlier I Enoch, though sharing the fallen angels tradition. It is referred to as Slavonic since

the only full copy of the text was in Church Slavonic, presumably translated from the Greek. The surviving texts are late, dated from the fourteenth to eighteenth century CE and, as a result, contain interpolated material. There are two recensions of 2 Enoch, a short and a long, both of which contain additions and neither of which can be considered pristine. The source of the Greek text most probably lies in Alexandria and an urban Jewish diaspora: a distinctly different background to the Diadochan wars that bore so heavily on the compositor of 1 Enoch. Consequently, it does not express the same anti-Hellenism.

As a pseudepigraphic text, 2 Enoch was of importance not to Judaism, but to the Christian community, particularly in monastic circles where it was disseminated. The Watchers/Satan sections that I will examine are based on the Aramaic (fragments) of 1 Enoch, though as with Jubilees, it assimilates different strains, and arguably, later Bogomil teachings.

2 Enoch was first published in Russian, in the mid nineteenth century, and subsequently in English in 1896 by R. H. Charles and W. R. Morfill. The fallen angel 'traditions' in modern witchcraft would appear to date to the interest sparked by the late publication of this and 1 Enoch, rather than any lineal survival.[8] I will cite F. I. Andersen's translation, as it supercedes the previous editions.

The narrative for the fall in 2 Enoch is given in 29:4–6 and markedly relies on Isaiah 14:12. Here the Lucifer mytheme and that of the fallen angels are bound together:

> But one from the order of Archangels deviated, together with the division that was under his authority. He thought up the impossible idea that he might place his throne higher than the clouds which are above the earth, that he might become equal to my power. And I hurled him out from the height, together with his angels. And he was flying around in the air, ceaselessly above the bottomless [abyss].

In Isaiah a king is denied the proper burial rites, and thus stellar ascension; here, the rival figure is allowed to take flight, but is confined to the sublunary sphere. The transformation from doomed king to rival angel is complete. He flutters in the lower heavens, accompanied, not by the mighty dead, but by a retinue of errant spirits.

In 2 Enoch 18:3 (long version) as Enoch ascends to heaven, in the manner of the Merkabah mystics, he sees the 200 angels, the grigori (watchers), and their leader, who is named as Satanail. Satanail is Satan, with the suffix 'ail/el' appended to demarcate his angelic heritage. This constitutes a deliberate shift from Asael/Šemhazah, to position the fallen angels narrative within the ambit of the Adamic story.[9] This displacement locates the genesis of evil in the body of Satan, as serpent in the garden of Eden. It is his first breach into the Enoch books. 2 Enoch continues the Adamic approach, telling the origin story where Satan and his angels refuse to worship Adam and are thus expelled from heaven; their motive established, they seek revenge upon him and all future generations. A similar teaching is found in the Qur'an. Such a theology removes the difficulty of an ambiguous God who tasks the fallen cohorts to beleaguer man.

Even if, as noted in the introduction to this chapter,[10] Satanail is a late addition, the Adamic material is not. The two competing accounts for the origin of evil – one in the garden and one with the descent of the angels – is where it is tempting to cleave Lucifer and Satan. Conversely, 2 Enoch shows that theology (and heresy) consistently sought to demonstrate their unity. Traces of the Adamic Bogomil doctrine are preserved in 2 Enoch 31:3–8: (italics mine)

> The devil understood how I wished to create another world, so that everything could be subjected to Adam on the earth, to rule and reign over it. The devil is of the lowest places. *And he will become a demon, because he fled from heaven; Sotona, because his name was Satanail.* In this way he became different from the angels. His nature did not change, but his thought did, since his consciousness of righteous and sinful things changed. And he became aware of his condemnation and of the sin which he sinned previously. And that is why he thought up the scheme against Adam. In such

a form he entered paradise, and corrupted Eve. But Adam he did not contact. But on account of her nescience [ignorance] I cursed them. But those whom I had blessed previously, them I did not curse...neither mankind I cursed, nor the earth, nor any other creature, but only mankind's evil fruit bearing. That is why the fruit of doing good is sweat and exertion.

Andersen detects a slavonic pun in the words for 'demon' (*běsi*) and 'fled' (*běže*). It is certainly suggestive of the etymology for the light-fleeing Lucifuge of Psellus and *Le Grand Grimoire*. The textual complexity is augmented with the naming of Satanail/Sotona, a play on the word for 'to make, to create.' The Devil/demon –who is named as such because he fled – created his own lower heaven. It can be reasonably surmised that this is a Bogomil insertion as there are no futher mentions of Satanail in the book and the puns are not translations, they work only in the Slavonic.

Several manuscripts of 2 Enoch contain yet another tradition, relating the descent of three watchers to Ermon (Mount Hermon); a teaching which is also found in the circa fifth century CE *Sefer Hekhalot*, designated as 3 Enoch. In this late text they are named as 'Uzzah, 'Azzah, and 'Aza'el. *Sefer Hekhalot* 5 gives the watchers a role as teachers that upholds the tradition of 1 Enoch:

What did the men of Enosh's (Enoch) generation do? They roamed the world from end to end... They brought down the sun, the moon, the stars and the constellations... How was it that they had the strength to bring them down? It was only because 'Uzzah, 'Azzah, and 'Aza'el taught them sorceries that they brought them down and employed them, for otherwise they would not have been able to bring them down.

3 Enoch and 2 Enoch relate the Adamic with the Enochic, initiating a trajectory that steadily ascends into Enoch/Metatron and Merkabah mysticism. Importantly, these texts illustrate how later discourses on Satan and the Adamic tradition were woven from the

warp and weft of 1 Enoch, and further, that their design consciously replicates the Lucifer motif of Isaiah 14:12 via 'the prince of the power of the air' of Ephesians 2:2.

The *Apocalypse of Abraham*, which is dated to 70–150 CE, survives only in Slavonic, although composed originally in Hebrew. The book attacks idol worship and polytheism, thereby providing a record of these practices. Fascinatingly, for our purposes, it presents an encounter with a fallen angel. The apocalypse section is an expansion of Genesis 15:8–17, wherein Abraham is commanded to perform a sacrifice on Mount Horeb – the site where Moses received the Ten Commandments – which necessitates a journey of forty days.[11] He is guided on his pilgrimage by an angel. Genesis 15:11 renders the scene of sacrifice, 'And when the fowls came down upon the carcases, Abram drove them away.' The word used for 'fowls/birds of prey' in Hebrew is עיט (*ayit*) meaning pointedly 'to scream, cry.' Such a bird is designated unclean, leading to the logical assumption that these are carrion eaters, whether eagles, kites or vultures,[12] and hence if they feed on the sacrifice, they will despoil it. Given the identification of the Rephaim with birds of prey, it seems secure to state that the writer of the *Apocalypse of Abraham*, who repeats the event, is attacking a persistent complex of cultic forms, from idolatry to the ancestor cult. The implication is that sacrifice was once made to these 'angels.' Mark 1:26 offers evidence of continuity in the identification of gods/ mighty dead/angels/demons with unclean birds and their cries, 'And when the unclean spirit had torn him, and cried with a loud voice, he came out of him.' As is typical of the New Testament, the context is that of the exorcism of a spirit. Certainly, this tradition continued in the *Lemegeton*, whose spirit throng contains a significant number of unclean birds.

Chapter 13 of the *Apocalypse of Abraham* furnishes us with additional information: the bird of prey is named as Azazel. It reveals that the writer is familiar with the Enochic literature, although the extent to which he is drawing on an Enochic tradition, or extemporising, is open to debate. But clearly the fallen angels were considered as robed like the feathered dead, whether kingly eagles, wedge tailed kites, or dread vultures. Distinct from the mute encounter of Genesis, in the *Apocalypse of Abraham* a dialogue ensues between man and watcher and angel. Azazel challenges Abraham, saying:

> What doest thou, Abraham, upon the Holy Heights, where no man eateth or drinketh, neither is there upon them any food of man, but these [beings] consume everything with fire and will burn thee up. Forsake the man [i.e. the angel] who is with thee, and flee, for if thou ascendest to the Heights, they will make an end of thee...

Azazel blocks the heavenward flight of Abraham, who has fasted in preparation for his ascent, and cautions that the angel is deceiving him and will lead him to his doom. A reversal of the tradition where the eagle takes the hero up to the heavens, as in the Etana story. Notably, the angel has been anthropomorphised, and it is Azazel who assumes the form of the now diabolised eagle. The angel intercedes, demanding Azazel leave, recounting the tale of the fallen angels as justification:

> Depart from this man! Thou canst not lead him astray, because he is an enemy to thee, and of those who follow thee and love what thou willest. For, behold, the vesture which in heaven was formerly thine hath been set aside for him, and the mortality which was his hath been transferred to thee. The Angel said to me: [...] Say to him: Be thou the burning coal of the furnace of the earth; go, Azazel, into the inacessible parts of the earth; [...] And the angel said to me: Answer him not, for God hath given him power over those who do answer him. And however much he spake to me, I answered nothing whatsoever.

I have not included the disputed sections of this passage, which may be Bogomil interpolations; they are indicated by square brackets and appended in the endnote.[13] Even without them, features of medieval demonology are presaged, expressly, the danger of conversing with spirits. Abraham and his angel then ascend to heaven on the backs of doves, in contrast to the ascent on eagles of their pagan counterparts.

It is often supposed that the Enochic tradition was purged or covered up in Christianity. Whilst this view may add glamour to 'magical history,' it does not match the evidence. We must remember that Christianity was, for an extended period, indistinguishable from Judaism and carried within it a fascination with the variant Enochic strains. They played into the emergent apocalyptic eschatology of Christ the Saviour. Indeed, the early Church Fathers, Irenaeus, Tertullian and Origen, supported the inclusion of the Enochic material precisely because it was valued in Judaism.

It seems highly probable that the Enochic family of texts, or their tradition, was known to the pseudepigraphical writer of 2 Peter 2:4, 'God spared not the angels that sinned, but cast them down to hell, and delivered them into chains of darkness, to be reserved unto judgment.' Though arguably this could come from a reading of Jude 1:6, 'And the angels which kept not their first estate, but left their own habitation, he hath reserved in everlasting chains under darkness unto the judgment of the great day.' What can be securely stated is that in the theological tumult that birthed Christianity, the fallen angels tradition was being drawn upon; it had not been anathemised. Revelation, in particular, is replete with Enochian motifs; they have so marked the final apocalypse of John that without (re)cognising them, a difficult text is rendered impenetrable. Therefore, though the Enochian books were eventually removed as discrete units, their memetic survival was guaranteed by the inclusion of their formulae in the coda of Revelation.

It was Augustine who eventually condemned the Enochic material, in his 410 CE *City of God*, on the grounds that its provenance was not secure, and henceforth it was excluded from the canon:

But it is not without reason that these writings have no place in that canon of Scripture which was preserved in the temple of the

Hebrew people by the diligence of successive priests; for their antiquity brought them under suspicion, and it was impossible to ascertain whether these were his genuine writings, and they were not brought forward as genuine by the persons who were found to have carefully preserved the canonical books by a successive transmission. So that the writings which are produced under his name, and which contain these fables about the giants, saying that their fathers were not men, are properly judged by prudent men to be not genuine; just as many writings are produced by heretics under the names both of other prophets, and more recently, under the names of the apostles, all of which, after careful examination, have been set apart from canonical authority under the title of Apocrypha.[14]

The Christians were following the example of Judaism, which for similar reasons – antiquity and dubious paternity – had begun to quietly exclude the Enoch material. Augustine's verdict is given further context when we note that the *Book of Giants* was considered scripture by the Manicheans, a rival group whom Christianity defined itself in opposition to. The Manichean *Book of Giants* is an Enochic text; from the surviving fragments it appears to be based heavily on I Enoch. Such a brief mention of Manichaeism may seem unjust, but it adds little to the Lucifer narrative beyond its role as antagonist to the Church. Christianity definitively shifted the pivot of Genesis to the story of Adam and Eve: the serpent and Devil deployed as a propaganda tool in the conquest of paganism, the angels fated to the realm of disquieting shadows.

Two gnostic texts that reference the fallen angels are known from the discoveries at Nag Hammadi: the *Apocryphon of John* and *On the Origin of the World*. The first, also known as the *Secret Book of John*, curiously places the angelic descent after the flood. The angels here are shapeshifters and seducers:

The angels changed their appearance to look like the partners of these women and filled the women with the spirits of darkness that they had concocted, and with evil... The angels took women, and from the darkness they produced children similar to their spirit. They closed their minds and became stubborn through the stubbornness of the contemptible spirit until the present day.

By contrast, in *On the Origin of the World* the fallen angels are deviant teachers, created by the seven rulers of darkness (an unorthodox inclusion), and with the new development of a soteriological figure, 'the true man':

Now, when the seven rulers were cast down from their heavens onto the earth, they made for themselves angels, numerous, demonic, to serve them. And the latter instructed mankind in many kinds of error and magic and potions and worship of idols and spilling of blood and altars and temples and sacrifices and libations to all the spirits of the earth, having their shared fate, who came into existence by the concord between the gods of injustice and justice.

And thus when the world had come into being, it distractedly erred at all times. For all men upon earth worshipped the spirits (demons) from the creation to the consummation – both the angels of righteousness and the men of unrighteousness. Thus did the world come to exist in distraction, in ignorance, and in a stupor. They all erred, until the appearance of the true man.

Both these works draw on 1 Enoch 6–11, Genesis 6:1–4 and Jubilees whilst freely extemporising from them.

The *Testament of Reuben*, from the Testaments of the Twelve Patriarchs, is a second century CE work; it is evidently derivative, based on Genesis and the Enochic corpus. It confirms that Enochic speculation persisted even after Augustine. Furthermore, it uses the Watcher story as a homily on lust, the root of which is identified as woman:

For evil are women, my children; and since they have no power or strength over man, they use wiles by outward attractions, that they may draw him to themselves. And whom they cannot bewitch by outward attractions, him they overcome by craft. For moreover, concerning them, the angel of the Lord told me, and taught me, that women are overcome by the spirit of fornication more than men, and in their heart they plot against men; and by means of their adornment they deceive first their minds, and by the glance of the eye instill the poison, and then through the accomplished act they take them captive. For a woman cannot force a man openly, but by a harlot's bearing she beguiles him. Flee, therefore, fornication, my children, and command your wives and your daughters, that they adorn not their heads and faces to deceive the mind: because every woman who useth these wiles hath been reserved for eternal punishment. For thus they allured the Watchers who were before the flood; for as these continually beheld them, they lusted after them, and they conceived the act in their mind; for they changed themselves into the shape of men, and appeared to them when they were with their husbands. And the women lusting in their minds after their forms, gave birth to giants, for the Watchers appeared to them as reaching even unto heaven. Beware, therefore, of fornication; and if you wish to be pure in mind, guard your senses from every woman.

The Watchers are now entirely disincarnate, and are relegated to the world of thoughts, the very opposite of the embodied angels of Jubilees. Even their stature is now an astral form, the idea of physical giants spiritised. They are the aerial projections of female wantonness, summoned by the magical arts of cosmetics and jewellery – which are to become symbola of the witch, the harlot and, of course, the Whore of Babylon. Perhaps here we have an etiology for 'un-natural' births as the result of the mental imprint taken in coitus: a formula familiar to practitioners of sex magic.

The Testaments of the Twelve Patriarchs was popularised in Europe as a Latin translation in the thirteenth century, before falling out of favour in the sixteenth when its provenance was cast into doubt. These were ideas which surely informed the demonologists' conception of the demonic female in league with the fallen angels, and Lucifer/Satan/the Devil.

Man and woman were divided against each other, as surely as Adam and Eve were by her intrigue with the serpent: a theological position bolstered by the teachings of St Paul. The inner, closed world of woman was viewed with absolute suspicion[15] as harbouring erotic thought crimes. Even when in the conjugal embrace of her husband, demonic deception and conception could occur. Orgasm was therefore to be shunned. Woman, in this reading, becomes not victim, but witch, whose womb seethes with potential unborn astral interlopers. Given the popularity of this text in the early modern period, it is a notable instance of the Watcher story influencing the authors of the witch hunts and the authors of the witch hunting manuals. Though the text had fallen out of favour when the fever was at its peak, the misogynist discourse of The Testament of the Twelve Patriarchs cannot have failed to leave its mark on the landscape and mindset of Europe. With the Church seeking to suppress the internal threat of female mystics, the fallen angel story could be used as an argument for the inherent susceptibility of woman to demonic incursion.

The final text I will consider is the third century CE *Clementine Homilies*, a novelised account of Clement's conversion to Christianity, the teachings of Peter and the refutation of Simon Magus (thence becoming a source for the Faustus legend). It was a popular text in the Middle Ages in Latin translation, for both monastic and lay audiences. Once again it demonstrates how the fallen angels, even in the absence of I Enoch, continued to inform folk belief and the popular imagination. Homily 8:12 relates the 'Metamorphoses of the Angels': (italics mine)

> For of the spirits who inhabit the heaven, the angels who dwell in the lowest region, being grieved at the ingratitude of men to

God, asked that they might come into the life of men, that, really becoming men, by more intercourse they might convict those who had acted ungratefully towards Him, and might subject every one to adequate punishment. When, therefore, their petition was granted, they metamorphosed themselves into every nature; for, being of a more godlike substance, they are able easily to assume any form. *So they became precious stones, and goodly pearl, and the most beauteous purple, and choice gold, and all matter that is held in most esteem.* And they fell into the hands of some, and into the bosoms of others, and suffered themselves to be stolen by them. They also changed themselves into beasts and reptiles, and fishes and birds, and into whatsoever they pleased.[16] These things also the poets among yourselves, by reason of fearlessness, sing, as they befell, attributing to one the many and diverse doings of all.

In this passage, the angels assume physical forms and are, moreover, transformed into objects of desire. These are chosen for their significance, they recall 1 Timothy 2:9, 'In like manner also, that women adorn themselves in modest apparel, with shamefacedness and sobriety; not with braided hair, or gold, or pearls, or costly array.' These are repeated in the portrait of the Great Whore given in Revelation 17:4, 'And the woman was arrayed in purple and scarlet colour, and decked with gold and precious stones and pearls, having a golden cup in her hand full of abominations and filthiness of her fornication.' Given that Timothy and Revelation were composed in a similar timeframe, it is no surprise that they draw on a common repository of imagery. It is these which *Homilies* echoes; precious stones, gold, pearls and purple. Such splendours refer in general to the vanity of women, but the components have more precise allegorical purposes. Purple is the colour of Imperial Rome and of the dye produced by the Phoenicians, evoking the fallen figure of the King of Tyre. The robe is the body that conceals spirit, or functions as glamour. Gold represents kingship and material power, as opposed to the atemporal reign of the crowned and conquering Christ child. The repetition of precious stones is directed against the widespread use of magical 'gnostic' gems, rings and stones, often considered to be of spermatic origin. Both gold and precious stones are revealed by Asael in 1 Enoch. These represent both covetousness and daimons enthroned in necklaces and rings. Pearls are an attribute of the love goddess, associated with wisdom and gnostic heresy, see in particular the Hymn of the Pearl.[7] Scripture is not consistent regarding the symbolism of precious stones; whilst viewed positively in accounts such as Matthew 7:6 and 13:45–6, or the jewelled paradises visited by Ezekiel and Enoch, in Kings and Chronicles precious stones are associated with the Queen of Sheba, and thus Solomon's fall into apostasy.

This opens an heretical perspective onto Revelation 17:4, gifting us a contemporary magical application whereby the adornments of Babalon embody the spirits of the fallen angels. The enchantment of magical jewellery has always been of considerable benefit to the witch or magician, as part of an *amorium/armorium*. The subtle change of emphasis is that the materia magica are the crystalised spirits who can be awoken, not the usual understanding that an unattached spirit is conjured into residing in a sympathetic setting. I have not exhausted the potential of this passage, to do so would be to anticipate the following volume, *Praxis*. However, meditation upon the image of the goddess described in Revelation will reveal further bodily mysteries and their talismanic reflexes.

Homily 8:13 continues, conveying the carnal nature of 'The Fall of the Angels':

> But when, having assumed these forms, they convicted as covetous those who stole them, and changed themselves into the nature of men, in order that, living holily, and showing the possibility of so living, they might subject the ungrateful to punishment, yet having become in all respects men, they also partook of human lust, and being brought under its subjection they fell into cohabitation with women; and being involved with them, and sunk in defilement and altogether emptied of their first power, were unable to turn back to the first purity of their proper nature, their

members turned away from their fiery substance: for the fire itself, being extinguished by the weight of lust, and changed into flesh, they trode the impious path downward. For they themselves, being fettered with the bonds of flesh, were constrained and strongly bound; wherefore they have no more been able to ascend into the heavens.

This homily makes the fall of the angels an allegory for the descent of spirit into matter. The divine nature is trapped, as in the gnostic teaching of the Sophia, in the matrix of flesh. The fall is the result of sex, making the fall of the angels equivalent to that of the fall in Eden. Women are shown as the source of contagion that prevents heavenly ascent. In this, Christianity has inverted the older tradition, that woman/the goddess is instrumental in the flight to heaven. The angels are bound by their weakness, a result of seminal emission and the pollution of women, with the tacit acknowledgement of the menstrual blood taboo.

Homily 8:14: 'Their Discoveries' pursues this line of exegesis, blending it gracefully with the 1 Enoch tradition that links the angels to the teaching of metallurgy and adornment: (italics mine)

For after the intercourse, being asked to show what they were before, and being no longer able to do so, on account of their being unable to do aught else after their defilement, yet wishing to please their mistresses, instead of themselves, they showed the *marrow* of the earth; I mean, the *flowers* of metals, gold, brass, silver, iron, and the like, with all the most precious stones. And along with these charmed stones, they delivered the arts of the things pertaining to each, and imparted the discovery of magic, and taught astronomy, and the powers of roots, and whatever was impossible to be found out by the human mind; also the melting of gold and silver, and the like, and the various dyeing of garments. And all things, in short, which are for the adornment and delight of women, are the discoveries of these demons bound in flesh.

The arts of the demons are manifestly the arts of women, in a profoundly antifeminist discourse. Here too, *Homilies* is reliant on I Enoch, repeating the teachings almost verbatim. It expands this somewhat to encompass the lapidiary and amuletic arts, by way of charmed stones. Gnostic gems were a pressing concern, as they were in wide use as personal phylacteries. Even the ensorcelling of fabric and garments through the art of dyeing can be inferred.

I have found no comment or critique of this passage that recognises the coded and oblique reference to a physical, energetic and sex magical technology known to its author. The Western equivalent to kundalini, the serpent power, is concealed beneath two words: namely, 'marrow' and 'flower.' Having expended themselves in lust, the angels show women the marrow of the earth. This is no mere metaphor, it is the use of precise technical (that is, initiatic) language. The sin and the effect are consanguineous. Marrow refers to the spinal marrow, specifically the cerebrospinal fluid, which manifests in women as menstrual blood and in men as semen. In revealing this I am not engaging in idle speculation, but drawing on a corpus of Orphic, Platonic and Gnostic literature that describes the magical body in terms that the writer of *Homilies* is clearly familiar with. Later in the text, in Homily 10:10: 'Idolatry, a Delusion of the Serpent,' we find a further proof that 'marrow' is used in a very specific sense, and with reference to its esoteric genealogy: (italics mine)

> For His alone is the excellent glory of being alone uncreated, while all else is created. As, therefore, it is the prerogative of the uncreated to be God, so whatever is created is not God indeed. Before all things, therefore, you ought to consider the evil-working suggestion of *the deceiving serpent that is in you, which seduces you by the promise of better reason, creeping from your brain to your spinal marrow*, and setting great value upon deceiving you.

The body leads us into sin, not as would be expected by means of the appetites, but by way of the serpent *within* the human body. And where is this serpent to be found? 'Creeping from your brain to your spinal marrow.' For the Christians, this inner teacher is not to be trusted. In the 'occult' anatomy (occult in the sense that it is internal, thus concealed), marrow is fed by the brain. The implications of this gnosis will flower in the following pages, and naturally, in *Praxis*.

The uncreated God is the invisible deity of the Deuteronomists. As we are created beings, we cannot, in Clement's opinion, be equal to or embody the divine. For the writer of *Homilies* the body deceives, as do the godmen and magicians of the gnostic sects, such as Simon Magus and Apollonius of Tyana. Lest this be considered an error, or a singular account, the Clementine *Recognitions* 5:17 repeats the doctrine:

> Above all, therefore, you ought to understand the deception of the old serpent and his cunning suggestions, who deceives you so to speak by prudence, and as by a sort of reason creeps through your senses; and beginning at the head, he glides through your inner marrow, accounting the deceiving of you a great gain.

The Clementine fear of ejaculation is reminiscent of the Chinese concern with depleting jing, or vital essence. But there is no need to go so far afield for evidence, nor are we reliant on theTantric tradition at this time, except for comparative purposes. Origen's self castration is a radical method of combatting semen loss and foiling demonic seduction. Some gnostic sects took the opposite approach, engaging in spermophagy. The question then arises, from which earlier tradition did these practices, both inhibitory and excitatory, arise?

In Plato's *Timaeus*,[18] we hear how soul power is a moist substance located in the brain which is connected to the penis by a channel running the length of the spine.[19] This is the exact anatomy that Clementine recounts. The *Timaeus* further betrays knowledge of *ida* and *pingala*, the channels that run the length of the spine, crossing at vital points.[20] The soul fluid is lost in ejaculation and therefore the philosopher must aim to prevent such leakage. Plato was almost certainly relying on the Pythagorean and Orphic traditions of Magna Graecia, present day Southern Italy, circa the fifth century BCE. The word for the marrow being *aiōn*,[21] life, a name for Dionysos. A comparable understanding of aiōn is encountered in Homer – where it is linked with *psychē* – which permits us to place this conception as current in Greece in 1500 BCE. Tracing these ideas, of the serpent power in the head and spine and the crossing points of ida and pingala, takes the origin back to the entwined serpents on the Sumerian Gudea vase circa 2300 BCE. Thus the Clementine recension of occult anatomy has significantly ancient roots, arguably reaching beyond the head cults of the Stone Age to a distant Pangaean source. E. J. Michael Witzel[22] observes that this force, which manifests as heat that rises up the spine, 'is a very old Pan-Gaean trait,' and further, that 'the concept of shamanic heat, and the careful management of this "power," which (snakelike) moves up the spine, is a fact still known to Yogic practitioners.' Iconographic and textual evidence, particularly as discussed by Thomas McEvilley, shows that knowledge of the serpent within was not limited to the Indian subcontinent. Indeed, as we have seen, this knowledge persisted in guarded form in the writings of the Church Fathers, where the assimilation of the spinal serpent to the serpent in the garden was effected.

The connection of serpent, marrow and the dead is preserved by Aelian (175–235 CE) in his De natura animalium I.51. He seems not entirely sure of his material, but records it nonetheless:

> The spine of a dead man, they say, transforms the putrefying marrow into a snake. The brute emerges, and from the gentlest of beings crawls forth the fiercest. Now the remains of those that were fine and noble are at rest and their reward is peace, even as the soul also of such men has the rewards which wise men celebrate in their songs. But it is from the spine of evildoers that such evil monsters are begotten even after life. The fact is, the whole story is either a fable, or if it is to be relied upon as true, then the corpse of a wicked man receives (so I think) the reward of his ways in becoming the progenitor of a snake.

Aelian, it must be remembered, is far removed from the Greek hero cults, the *lares familiares* and the benefic archaic tradition of the serpent. The work of Aelian becomes a source for the bestiaries of the medieval period, so too does that of Pliny and Tacitus where the marrow and serpent become the progenitor of a more familiar emblem of resurrection, the phoenix.

The conception of the heroic dead as serpents is dramatically illustrated in the work of Plutarch (46–120 CE), as he relates the death of the Spartan King in 'Cleomenes' 39.1–3:

> And a few days afterwards those who were keeping watch upon the body of Cleomenes where it hung, saw a serpent of great size coiling itself about the head and hiding away the face so that no ravening bird of prey could light upon it. In consequence of this, the king was seized with superstitious fear, and thus gave the women occasion for various rites of purification, since they felt that a man had been taken off who was of a superior nature and beloved of the gods. And the Alexandrians actually worshipped him, coming frequently to the spot and addressing Cleomenes as a hero and a child of the gods; but at last the wiser men among them put a stop to this by explaining that, as putrefying oxen breed bees, and horses wasps, and as beetles are generated in asses which are in the like condition of decay, so human bodies, when the juices about the marrow collect together and coagulate, produce serpents. And it was because they observed this that the ancients associated the serpent more than any other animal with heroes.

The account of Plutarch is of interest as it contains both the archaic tradition, notably continued by the women who preside over mourning rites, and the rationalising response of 'wise men.'

By such routes, the significance of marrow continued to be known in Europe. Shakespeare includes it in several plays and poems. Spending semen as marrow dries out the bones in the lecher in

Antony and Cleopatra I.iv.27; and in *Venus and Adonis* 142–3, the desire of Venus is a warm wet fire – she proclaims, 'My flesh is soft and plump, my marrow burning, My smooth soft hand, were it with thy hand felt, Would in thy palm dissolve or seem to melt.' The language of liquifying or melting can be found in Homer, Empedocles and the Orphics. It is not mere lubricity, but is an emanation of seed from the brain and marrow. The seed, according to Aristotle, is a liqour that originates in the head, and around the eyes in particular; the seat of risen kundalini. The word he uses for this substance, the cerebro-spinal fluid/marrow, is aiōn.[23] To be cognisant of the complex of associations around the aiōn perforce transforms the limited understanding of the *kalas*, which are too often considered as nectars bereft of origin beyond their outflowing in the flower chalice of the female sex. They must be distilled, periodically. A purely genital approach to sex magic ignores the dynamic relationship of skull seat, spine and pelvic girdle in the cultivation of vital essence. It is indicative of the current tendency to disarticulate the body.

The Clementine account of the fallen angels can thus be read as a warning against the folly of seminal emission. It would appear that de Sade, in poetically describing the ejaculate as 'angelic discharge,' with characteristic anti-clerical flourish, was well within the bounds of Christian teaching. The 'deceiving wisdom' that the Church Fathers warned against is explicitly imparted to women, and thence to men, as an angelic discourse on the art of sex.

The four hundred year absence of the books of Enoch from the Western tradition has spawned much speculation. However, whilst the texts were excluded, the stories were not – they were carried in Genesis and Revelation, in the oral Jewish tradition, in late texts such as The Testament of the Twelve Patriarchs, and transmitted through the various heresies that fomented in the Balkans to spread throughout Europe.

The fallen angels are the founding myth of witchcraft, a verdict that neopaganism is loath to recognise. But the sins of the daughters of men is the witchcraft etiology that the Church dogmatically pursued, at times combined with the dramatic exchange in the Garden of Eden and Eve as first witch. Such is our history. The record is preserved in the witch hunting manuals, as a reading of the *Malleus Maleficarum* demonstrates.[24] When women are derided for their carnal lust, an original transgression is summoned. Sprenger and Kramer did not innovate, but repeated the verdict of the Church Fathers, drawing on the authority of Genesis 6:1–4; they wrote:

> we may say with St Augustine that it is true that all the superstitious arts had their origin in a pestilent association of men with devils.

> Devils know how to ascertain the virtue in semen: first, by the temperament of him from whom the semen is obtained; secondly, by knowing what woman is most fitted for the reception of that semen; thirdly, by knowing what constellation is favourable to that corporeal effect; and we may add, fourthly, from their own words we learn that those whom they beget have the best sort of disposition for devils' work. When all these causes so concur, it is concluded that men born in this way are powerful and big in body.

Remarkably, the *Malleus* alludes to the existence of sex magical techniques, in particular the importance of the constellations, that is, the home of the deified ancestors. It is the forbidden antediluvian stellar wisdom of the watchers, preserved by Cainan and his line. Remarkably, the men born as a result of this congress are described as giants, like the Nephilim.

> Therefore, to return to the question whether witches had their origin in these abominations, we shall say that they originated from some pestilent mutual association with devils, as is clear from our first knowledge of them. But no one can affirm with certainty that they did not increase and multiply by means of these foul practices, although devils commit this deed for the sake not of pleasure but of corruption.

Witchcraft is perpetuated by a spirit process that is given in detail:

> A Succubus devil draws the semen from a wicked man; and if he
> is that man's own particular devil, and does not wish to make
> himself an Incubus to a witch, he passes that semen on to the
> devil deputed to a woman or witch; and this last, under some
> constellation that favours his purpose that the man or woman so
> born should be strong in the practice of witchcraft, becomes the
> incubus of that witch.

The incubus here seems to be a spirit familiar to the witch, or her
spirit lover; it is ambiguous. The familiar spirit is a particularly notable feature in early modern accounts of English witchcraft. Trans-
vection to the sabbat is often accomplished by riding the familiar,
who can also play the part of personal devil and sexual partner at the
celebration. The grimoire analogue is the intermediary spirit, with
whom the sorceror must first form a pact.

The gnostic focus on semen and the stellar wisdom necessary for
the selection of a nativity are likewise to be noted. The section ends
with an exegesis on Genesis 6:4:

> And it is no objection that those of whom the text speaks were not
> witches but only giants and famous and powerful men; for, as was
> said before, witchcraft was not perpetrated in the time of the law
> of Nature, because of the recent memory of the Creation of the
> world, which left no room for Idolatry. But when the wickedness
> of man began to increase, the devil found more opportunity to dis-
> seminate this kind of perfidy. Nevertheless, it is not to be under-
> stood that those who were said to be famous men were necessarily
> so called by reason of their good virtue.

The phrasing of the *Malleus* suggests sensitivity to the risk of
misreading the creation of the giants as beneficial. It further deals
with the dilemma that the offspring are not identified as witches,
though admittedly, not entirely successfully – perhaps because the

origin story is not supported by the canon alone, but relies upon oral transmission and texts such as Jubilees. A further possibility is the existence of heretical sects that did hold such a 'Luciferian' belief, or beliefs.

In the case of a proposed Luciferianism, the existence of such a sect would have been documented; there would be no benefit to underplaying such a group, in fact the opposite would be true. In the historical record there are indeed found groups who are described as 'Luciferian.' However, when examined, the term is deployed as part of the Church's attack on Bogomil and Cathar dualism: heresy and witchcraft were assimilated into a single enemy beneath a single leader. The Papal Bull of 1233, *Vox in Rama*,[25] is aimed at one such sect of purported Luciferians. It details an initiation and orgy with a black cat and a pale man with coal black eyes. These antics are followed with a summary of their supposed doctrine: Lucifer has been unjustly deposed; Lucifer is the true creator of heaven; God will be cast out and Lucifer restored. The heretics engage in acts which God hates, to the pleasure and glory of Lucifer. Norman Cohn demolishes such claims on the basis that they are merely repetitions of clerical attacks from the previous 400 years, sewn into a single garment. In the absence of further proof, such as authenticated tracts praising Lucifer and evidence not extracted under torture, it seems that Cohn's analysis will stand.[26]

Cohn cannot, however, credibly deny the possiblity of Luciferian beliefs; the manner in which gnostic thought generates copious and novel exegesis makes it almost unthinkable that individuals did not produce such a discourse – though I concur with him that an organised or persistent sect, that harboured a Luciferian ideology, did not exist. That the dualists did engage in speculation on Lucifer is attested by one Cathar story, recorded in the 1214 *De Heresi Catharorum*. In it, Lucifer (pre-fall) encounters a being with four faces, those of a man, bird, fish and beast. This being leads Lucifer astray, who in turn corrupts the angels. The four faces are those of the evangelists, and as Parpola might observe, the kerubim guardians of kingship. This tale seems more typical of the sort that Cathar theology would produce, rather than the untrammeled appetite for contrareity and carnality that that Church wished to foist upon them.

The absence in the historical record of a codified Luciferianism does not prevent such a heresy coming into being, inspired by such accounts and carefully applying elements of their ritual structures.

The Cloven Hoof

If Isaiah gives apotheosis; Leviticus the scapegoat; the Deuteronomists
limits upon kingship; Enoch teaching by divine beings; Jubilees the
sanctioned angel of hostility; then there is only one fatal aspect to
plot in the nativity: Satan. A darker angel enters the story as the cult
of Yahweh becomes not monolatrous, demanding the exclusive worship of one god, but monotheist, denying the existence of all other
gods. Although this process begins in Judaism, it is in the apocalyptic cult of Christianity where it fully blooms. Having attained such
dominance, God, in a sense, retreats from the field of action until
the final decisive conflict, envisaged in Revelation, and the prophesied return of Christ ushering in a Golden Age.

It is not without some trepidation that I broach the difficult
issue of Satan. In doing so I will tread with lighter foot, as Satan has
received much attention from both scholars and practitioners. In
telling the story of Lucifer, I do not intend to deny Satan his due;
my intent is to explore the way in which these characters both differ
and coincide. Though it may be desirable to ultimately cleave these
figures, it would be remiss not to outline their similarities and to ac-
knowledge that such a distinction was traditionally not drawn. The
twists and turns in this course will be charted in the transition from
Old to New Testament, the reckoning in Revelation and the works

of the Church Fathers. Ultimately, my suggestion is this: we would do better to consider Satan and Lucifer as a single entity with a cloven hoof. Perhaps, for ease of comprehension, one could consider this composite entity to be the Devil.

For some the inclusion of Satan in a study of Lucifer is a heresy in itself. Such a perspective regards Lucifer and Satan as separate entities, one of which is 'ours,' the secret chief of witchcraft and magic, and the other a Christian bogeyman and 'theirs.' This is a fallacious argument and scripture is clear on the matter: Satan is considered to be identical with Mastêmâ, Belial/Beliar, Azazel, Samael et al., and Lucifer. The exclusion of Satan is no better than the dualism which it purports to reject, only to enshrine in the very heart of its argument.

The biblical figure, the Satan, notably occurs in Job 1:6–2:7; 1 Chronicles 21:1, Zechariah 3:1–2, and Numbers 22:22–35. Here Satan means adversary or accuser; this is a function or office which becomes increasingly personified. Originally, the Satan was a member of the divine council who had a defined and divinely ordained role. Like Lucifer, he was an angel. Elsewhere in the Bible, 'Satan' is used in a more general sense to describe a political or military opponent.

As a folk figure, the Satan does not stand against God, he is an important functionary of his court, an instrument of divinity. Satan's existence removes culpability for suffering from the divine ruler and enables him to test the faith of his people without sullying himself. There is a similarity here between the Satan and the Watchers, as hand-and-eye operatives of the security state. Thus in Numbers, Satan is not the enemy of God but his messenger; in Job, Satan is an agent provocateur, not the evil angel of temptation. The difficulty occurs in the transition to monotheism with the overthrow and eclipse of the divine assembly. As a result, the Satan must be recast, the angel summarily flung from heaven. The gulf of plausible deniability becomes a yawning chasm into which Satan, the scapegoat for the sins of God, is condemned.

By absolving God from evil acts, Satan serves as an explanation for why good men suffer. And when the divine court is exiled, Satan bloats into the enemy of all creation. The rift between God and his heavenly assembly births a profoundly dualist universe for Satan and his cohorts to inhabit: a universe predicated on conflict. A cosmic lex talionis inevitably ensues, with the reassurance that the divine tyrant will triumph at the end of time, as he did in the beginning. In a sense, Satan runs amok amongst humanity. The creator god absents himself; perhaps, as the gnostics would whisper, senile, or even mad. The rise of Satan is theological blowback.

It was a small step to implicate the celestial Satan with the thwarted ascendancy of Hêlēl Ben Šaḥar, and the angelic rebellion of Genesis and Enoch, and in so doing, marshal a single narrative and a singular enemy.

The Satan material is a result of Second Temple Judaism asking the question: what is the nature and origin of evil? This is tied to the changing conception of Yahweh, the shadow of which we perhaps glimpsed in the Deuteronomists' reaction to the goat offered for Azazel. Answers posited to this thorny question comprised the corruption of humans by fallen angels (1 Enoch); evil as primordial chaos (Daniel); the disobedience of Adam and Eve (4 Ezra); and the inherent wickedness of the human heart (Genesis).

In the transition from Old to New Testament, Satan does not diminish, but grows in stature. Evidently, Satan is the opposer to the mission of Christ,[1] an enemy with many faces. In the New Testament, Satan and Devil – from the Greek διάβολος (diábolos, slanderer) – are used interchangeably. This semantic drift is very telling. No longer does Satan have an appointed role in the cosmic order, but must kick his heels and, with time on his hands, becomes a sophist deceiver with no redeeming qualities.

In the Synoptic Gospels (Matthew, Mark and Luke), another character is introduced: Beelzebub/Beelzeboul, who takes the role of Satan. The name is a deliberate slur on b'l zbl, Baal as lord of the underworld,[2] which links this name to the lord of the Rephaim, and thence Lucifer, as addressed previously. No longer is the realm of chthonic deities sought out for healing oracles, as in the Ugaritic Baal texts, rather, the shades of the dead are seen as aggressive possessing entities requiring urgent exorcism. Sheol, the grave, is dispossessed from its etymological source as 'the place of enquiry'³ of necromantic rites. The New Testament, though popularly assumed to be more benefic than the Old, is built on an unholy trinity of enmity, conflict and exorcism. Satan is found in 2 Corinthians 11:13-15, attempting to deceive the community with false teachings, and in 12:7, torments Paul himself. Incessant conflict – Christian piety being predicated on total spiritual warfare – makes it an extremely dangerous cult. The experiences of Paul and the early church where incubated in monastic communities that reinforced the sense of an ever present demonic threat. This laid the groundwork for all subsequent European demonology, and the way in which witchcraft and magic are framed.

How is it that an angel of light becomes the angel of darkness?⁴ The original explanation for this lies in the religious community of Qumran, and the influence of Zoroastrian and Persian dualism upon it. Christianity confounded the ur combat myth, in which light triumphs over darkness, and the illuminated figure of Hêlēl Ben Šaḥar. Satan was the inevitable grotesque result, a fallen king swathed in darkness who wars with the radiant lamb. Christ supplanted the role of morning star and with it, all the trappings of kingship that were previously used to identify Hêlēl Ben Šaḥar, thereby seeding much confusion between the two. Moreover, scripture had to accommodate an enemy who was identified in conflicting terms as both darkness and light. Christianity appealed to the earlier notion of divine kingship via a tortured genealogy back to the House of David to gain greater legitimacy for its godman. Such a reading of the Christ myth sanctified kings in medieval Europe. Political enemies were demonised; and rebellion was seen as a cosmic threat to be eradicated without mercy. Ironically, royalty preserved the old totem of kingship, the serpent or dragon, as testament to the enduring power of the archaic symbols.

Paul was mindful of the danger of heresy that confronted the nascent church, preaching in 2 Corinthians 11:14, 'And no marvel; for Satan himself is transformed into an angel of light.' Light itself becomes a source of deception. In the absence of a unified canon, rival readings, charismatic prophets, texts and exegesis vied for a congregation. Paul therefore made a distinction between true and false light, true and false vision.[5] The vexed issue of the nature of spirit and matter, light and darkness, became a battleground, and a persistent gnostic heresy whose suppression provided the raw material and atrocity stories that would be used to construct the case against witchcraft.[6]

In the New Testament the attributes of Hêlêl Ben Šaḥar, the story of the fall of the angels and the role of the accuser are thus blended into a single adversary who becomes the host of all the legends. This is what is read in Luke 10:18, 'And he said unto them, I beheld Satan as lightning fall from heaven.' The two myths and mythic figures are conjoined as the molten plasma breaches the heavens and strikes at the earth: Lucifer and Satan become a fused mass, like the glass faery castles of Ireland. When Satan is described as Legion, one can understand the term in the sense that he contains all forbidden discourses, that when undifferentiated present only a cacophony of smoke and noise. The light has been folded and folded and folded, until it has become indistinguishable from matter.

As Christianity left its birth place, the original polemical needs of Isaiah were displaced by fresh challenges and new adversaries. The horned gods of Old Europe are often cited in this respect: a convenient way to avoid tangling with the more ambiguous pan-European folk-devil figures that predate Christianity. The Murray thesis took this route, and Wicca went on to ostracise anti-clerical Satanism to make the budding nature religion palatable for the newspaper readers of middle England. Lucifer was not entirely absented, but presented via Charles Godfrey Leland's *Aradia* as a name for the Roman god of light, and coupled with the goddess Diana. It is soft focus scholarship at its worst.

Yet the problematic fusion of Lucifer and Satan, which pagan witchcraft sought to dispel, was solemnised in the final fateful book of the Bible, the one which preoccupied the Church as its power faded in the late Middle Ages. The book which is of critical relevance to witchcraft is Revelation. Any vestiges of a distinct Lucifer figure are lost, as his myths are drawn beyond the event horizon of Satan, and the last shreds of golden light used to glorify Christ.

Revelation is the repository for all the myths I have related, and is replete with Enochic references. It is most often compared with Daniel 7, but Daniel is itself reliant upon 1 Enoch. Such is the conclusion of Helge Kvanvig, who suggests that the compositor of Daniel 'was both acquainted with parts at least of the Book of Watchers in written form, and that he belonged to a milieu not far removed from the group behind this book.'[7]

The record of Enochic transmission is woven through the text of Revelation, beginning with the description of Jesus in 1:14, 'his head and his hairs were white like wool, as white as snow; and his eyes were as a flame of fire.' No comparable vision is to be found in the gospels, but it mirrors the image of the child Noah in the Book of Noah, 'and his body was white as snow and red as the blooming of a rose, and the hair of his head and his long locks were white as wool, and his eyes beautiful.'[8] The appearance of the apocalyptic Jesus is here given in kindred terms to the offspring of the angels: this new Messiah emerges in the iconography of a vanquished ancestor and his bloodline.

There are direct references to the fall of Lucifer; in Revelation 8:10 the star which falls is an allusion to the 'light bearer' of Isaiah 14:12, who is unfavourably compared with the lamp of God's word:

And the third angel sounded, and there fell a great star from heaven, burning as it were a lamp, and it fell upon the third part of the rivers, and upon the fountains of waters.[9]

In Revelation 9:1 the falling star image is repeated, and combined with it the eschatological motif of the release of the spirits from the pit. Thus Enoch and Isaiah are understood by John as comprising a unified narrative.

And the fifth angel sounded, and I saw a star fall from heaven unto the earth: and to him was given the key of the bottomless pit.

The imprisonment of the spirits is a repetition of Isaiah, Enoch and Leviticus: the liberation of evil is required for the final showdown with Christ and ultimate salvation. Such is the naked idea which would necessitate a plague of witches and sorcerers in early modern Europe – they were proofs of the immanence of the second coming.

The fall of the angels and their leader is retold in Revelation 12:9, in which their power is that of deception, a Satanic trick of the light, rather than an account of hubris or a teaching of forbidden knowledge. It is no mistake that the Devil and his angels are expelled from heaven in the manner that Adam and Eve are expelled from paradise:

> And the great dragon was cast out, that old serpent, called the Devil, and Satan, which deceiveth the whole world: he was cast out into the earth, and his angels were cast out with him.

The Eden story is clearly uppermost in John's mind as he equates the old serpent with Satan.[10] The Earth as chthonic and feminine is in opposition to the father god who has exiled even his court, the stars.

In Revelation, a mystery play is presented to the embattled Christian community: the number of characters has been drastically reduced, though the costumes that they wear are richly embroidered. It outlines a stark conflict of good versus evil, recognisable to those who had suffered under the oppression of Diocletian; it promised that this darkest of nights will presently be split by the rays of dawn. Revelation harks back to Genesis in search of meaning, and hope: it is to be expected, as *Urzeit* is in *Endzeit*, the first in the last, the *alpha* in the *omega*. John was not alone in believing that the ultimate plan of the Lord was encoded in Genesis. The New Testament abounds with references to the coming destruction of the world by fire, as a reflex to the first destruction by water. 2 Peter 3:10 is one such example, 'But the day of the Lord will come as a thief in the night; in the which the heavens shall pass away with a great noise, and the elements shall melt with fervent heat, the earth also and the works that are therein shall be burned up. John therefore stages his apocalypse as a Genesis masque, in a performance flooded in the light of the Enochic tradition. On the bare boards tread the players of the Christian mystery play, namely: Eve, Adam and the Serpent. Adam is Christ. The Serpent is the Devil, as leader of the fallen angels. Eve wears two masks: Madonna and Whore. God echoes off stage, a disembodied voice. The scene, recalling the ancient tragedy, is set by a rough wooden pole, a device that serves to indicate Eden, and by a lighting change Golgotha, where it can be pressed into service as the crucifix from which Christ steps down to deliver his verdict on the world.

The union of Lucifer and Satan, that John of Patmos presupposes, was blessed by the Church Fathers. Their writings were both theological and political, seeking in particular to refute the dualist Marcionite heresy. Origen was the first of the Fathers to make the connection between Satan and Hêlêl.[11] He brought together the diverse Old Testament references from Job, Ezekiel and Isaiah, and argued that Hêlêl, the King of Tyre, and the Leviathan of Job, were all identical with the Devil.[12] He used these texts to emphasise Satan's pride and his fall from heaven, and linked Hêlêl with the plasmatic emission of Satan in Luke 10:18. Later, Tertullian taught that before Satan's fall he was not only an angel, but the foremost angel. It is from the combined work of three theologians – Origen, Tertullian and Jerome – that the Lucifer mythos is canonised. In the first volume of *The Letters of St Jerome*, he writes:

> Lucifer fell, Lucifer who used to rise at dawn; and he who was bred up in a paradise of delight had the well-earned sentence passed upon him.

He then quotes scripture, the little remembered Obadiah,[13] verse 4:3, 'The pride of thine heart hath deceived thee, thou that dwellest in the clefts of the rock, whose habitation is high; that saith in his heart, Who shall bring me down to the ground?' Note that the cleft rock symbolism,[14] which is suggestive of pagan worship and the Ašerah cult, is attached to a paraphrasing of Isaiah. He continues, 'Though thou exalt thyself as the eagle, and though thou set thy nest among the stars, thence will I bring thee down, saith the Lord.' This may suggest familiarity with the legends of Zaphon/Kasios, though this is far from certain. It does recall the shamanic motif of flight that underlies the entire myth complex. Lucifer in aquiline form is multivalent, evoking Empire, cruelty, the Rephaim and Azazel as an unclean bird. Jerome then goes on to comment on Isaiah 14, 'Now the Sun of justice is rising in the West, but in the East, that notorious Lucifer, who had fallen, has exalted his throne above the stars.' This is a definitive oppositional reading of Christ and Lucifer as evening and morning stars, now serving as a Christian polemic. The East is demonised, with perhaps the Manichean heresy implied.

Origen, and later Augustine, believed that the Devil's envy arose from pride: the Devil envied God. Tertullian, on the other hand, suggested that the Devil was jealous of humans, believing that the Devil was furious that God had created humans in the divine image and had given them governance over the world. This is reminiscent of the refusal of the Qur'anic Iblis to bow to Adam (7:11).[15]

In Christian orthodoxy the Tertullian reading – Satan's jealousy of humans – ultimately lost out to that of Origen – his jealousy of God. Behind this struggle lies the Adamic material, a tradition that was preserved in the Qur'ān.

The Books of Adam date from the early Christian era and have a particularly gnostic cast, with Adam as the proto-Christ. The corpus includes the *Testament of Adam*, the *Life of Adam and Eve*, the *Apocalypse of Moses* and the *Apocalypse of Adam*. The emphasis on Adam was not a primary concern of Judaism but owes more to the Christian writings of Paul. The focus of the Adam books is upon Eden, and the conflict between Adam and Satan; the watcher story is implicit, but not centre stage. I consider the books as they demonstrate the iconographic consanguinity of Lucifer and Satan, upon whom they dwell.

In the *First Book of Adam and Eve* 7:9 the defiance of Satan is noted: Then the beasts did obeisance to Adam, according to the commandment of God; except the serpent, against which God was wroth. It did not come to Adam, with the beasts. Further details are given in the *Life of Adam and Eve* 14:1–16:2, wherein the serpent/angel speaks:

And Michael went out and called all the angels saying: 'Worship
the image of God as the Lord God hath commanded.' And
Michael himself worshipped first; then he called me and said:
'Worship the image of God the Lord.' And I answered, 'I have no
(need) to worship Adam.' And since Michael kept urging me to
worship, I said to him, 'Why dost thou urge me? I will not worship
an inferior and younger being (than I). I am his senior in the Creation, before he was made was I already made. It is his duty to worship me.' When the angels, who were under me, heard this, they
refused to worship him. And Michael saith, 'Worship the image of
God, but if thou wilt not worship him, the Lord God will be wrath
with thee.' And I said, 'If He be wrath with me, I will set my seat
above the stars of heaven and will be like the Highest.' And God
the Lord was wrath with me and banished me and my angels from
our glory; and on thy account were we expelled from our abodes
into this world and hurled on the earth.

The writer has carefully enfolded the account of Hêlêl in Isaiah into
the Adam story. The motif of the older not bowing to the younger
is that of Cain and Abel, employed as a challenge to Judaism and
Paganism to accept the superiority of the child Christ.

In the Georgian version of the text, Satan is disguised as an angel
of light: a Pauline motif. God reveals the deception in 27:12–14:

'O Adam, fear not. This is Satan and his hosts; he wishes to
deceive you as he deceived you at first. For the first time, he was
hidden in the serpent; but this time he is come to you in the
similitude of an angel of light; in order that, when you worshipped
him, he might enthrall you, in the very presence of God.' Then
the angel went from Adam, and seized Satan at the opening of the
cave, and stripped him of the feint he had assumed, and brought
him in his own hideous form to Adam and Eve; who were afraid of

him when they saw him. And the angel said to Adam, 'This hideous form has been his ever since God made him fall from heaven. He could not have come near you in it; therefore did he transform himself into an angel of light.'

The ugliness of the spirit is remembered in the grimoires, with the standard admonition: Show yourself in a fair and human shape. Monstrous appearance, a foul smell and noise are consistent with the clerical exorcism manuals.

In the late Adamic tradition Eve embarks on a tryst with Satan, the serpent. The fruit of their union is Cain; Abel is her son with Adam. The bloodline of Cain is notably extinguished by the flood; there are, thus, no surviving children of Cain. In the *Apocalypse of Moses* 19:1–3, Eve's sin is detailed:

And I opened to him and he walked a little way, then turned and said to me: 'I have changed my mind and I will not give thee to eat until thou swear to me to give also to thy husband.' (And) I said. 'What sort of oath shall I swear to thee? Yet what I know, I say to thee: By the throne of the Master, and by the Cherubim and the Tree of Life! I will give also to my husband to eat.' And when he had received the oath from me, he went and poured upon the fruit the poison of his wickedness, which is lust, the root and beginning of every sin, and he bent the branch on the earth and I took of the fruit and I ate.

Eve and the serpent is the earlier tradition, preceding that of Lilith and Adam: a tradition that can be dated to the c.7–10th century CE *Alphabet of ben Sira*, and was developed in subsequent medieval sources. It is interesting that their exchange between Lilith and Adam, in which she refuses to lie beneath, mirrors the non serviam stance of the serpent towards Adam. Lilith is assumed to be an early tradition due to the mention of לִילִית (*lilit*) in Isaiah 34:14, translated in the KJV as 'screech owl.' As my focus is very much on origins, I

have not deemed it necessary to look at the late Lilith/Samael material in this study, despite their increasing importance throughout the
medieval period.

The Adamic, like the Enochic, books, were excluded from the
canon, as Church doctrine shifted: Satan's pride was the result of
his envy of God, not his envy of Adam. The Devil's sin is *invidia*, a
sin of looking and coveting. For the Christians this was raised from
an action between individuals (often unconscious) to a conspiracy
against God himself. The power of the eye is cognate with fire and
light. Invidia, or the evil eye, is one of the oldest attested powers of
witchcraft. It was associated with the Telchines, legendary artificers
in brass and iron in ancient Greek mythology, reputed to be notorious magicians (*goëtes*) and bewitchers (*baskanoi*), literally those who
cast the evil eye. Invidia is expressly aimed at those in power: the
convex lens of the eye emitting fire at its target. It became a crime
most often ascribed to women, lack and weakness being constitu-
tional attributes of her kind. The persistence of this fear is evident
in Bacon's 1625 'Of Envy,' that, furthermore, compares the malign
stellar rays with the ray sent forth from the eye:

> ...We see, likewise, the Scripture
> calleth envy an evil eye, and the astrologers call the
> evil influences of the stars evil aspects, so that still there
> seemeth to be acknowledged, in the act of envy, an
> ejaculation or irradition of the eye; nay, some have
> been so curious as to note, that the times when the
> stroke or percussion of an envious eye doth most hurt,
> are when the party envied is beheld in glory or triumph,
> for that sets an edge upon envy; and, besides, at such
> times, the spirits of the person envied do come forth
> most into the outward parts, and so meet the blows.[16]

St Augustine, in his *Expositions on the Psalms*, regards Hêlēl enthroned on Zaphon and makes him his Satan; he then goes on to identify him as the serpent in Eden: For even as he who seduced him said of himself (i.e. Satan): I will set my throne towards the north, so likewise he persuaded Adam, saying: Taste and you shall be as gods. The satanising of the serpent, as I previously observed, was integral to the fight against gnostic heresy. Augustine notably makes the serpent culpable, rather than Eve.[17] The influence of Augustine on Western Christianity was profound.

In contrast, Theodoret of Cyrus (393–457 CE) brooked no confusion between Hêlēl and Satan, reading the fallen king as Nebuchadnezzar. It is a position still repeated today, despite evidence to the contrary. Theodoret is perhaps favouring Daniel, whose rebel king is a pasquinade on this monarch. The visceral and repulsive tone of his commentary on Isaiah 14:11 makes clear that the object of his mockery is a human king:

Although you aspired to heaven, he says, you have occupied the depths of the earth; instead of a sumptuous robe of purple, you have worms for vestment; instead of a soft couch you have decomposition and fetid pus.[18]

Luther and Calvin will likewise make no connection between Hêlēl and Satan when they come to examine the text. Nevertheless, Theodoret does understand 'morning star' to signify Lucifer, as an usurped name of God, and sees Satan standing behind Nebuchadnezzar. Commenting on Isaiah 14:12, he includes what becomes a common trope of Satan/Lucifer, that of illusion: Since, carried away with boastful imaginings, he [the King of Babylon] has aspired to ascend to heaven, he calls him 'morning star,' certainly not because he was, in truth, but because he had the illusion of so being.[19] The appeal to the illusory/doubling capacity of Satan/Lucifer was critical in disparaging the claims of rival godmen. Their miracles had to be placed in a different semantic category to those of Christ; even though they were in essence identical. As there was only one enemy, there could only be one saviour. Consequently, prominent figures, such as Simon Magus, were targeted; and magicians in toto were made the enemy of Christianity.

Theodoret is worth citing further, as he sets out the Christian reading of Isaiah when read in combination with Genesis and Enoch:

> Moreover, there was, it is said, a mountain in the North of the country of the Assyrians and the Medes, which separated them from the Scythian nations and was much more elevated than all the mountains in the world. It is by this [route] that without any doubt, that in all likelihood they had thought to attempt the ascent to heaven. But he had not been the only one to have this illusion: there had also been his master on the subject. And, if, figuratively, the conceit of this plan is applied to the king, it really applies to him who truly fell from the heavens, who had usurped the name of God and deceived the greater part of mankind.[20]

Theodoret's Hêlêl is the student of Satan: the conspirator behind all conspiracies. The ascent to heaven – whether constructed by Nimrod in Babylon, or dared by Hêlêl at Zaphon – was presented as having a unity of symbolic meaning and a singular inspiration.

The early Church Fathers likewise interpreted the fall of the King of Tyre in Ezekiel 28:11–19 as referring to Satan. Naturally, they drew on Jude 1:6, 2 Peter 2:4 and Revelation 9:1 and 12:9, by now familiar allusions. Just as Isaiah discusses the proper limits of kingship, so too does Ezekiel.[21] The King of Tyre is described in terms befitting the perfect monarch. The king in the ancient world was expected to be the image of virtue; for more on this in the Assyrian model see Parpola,[22] or indeed the example of Solomon. Consistently emphasised are his beauty and his wisdom. However, the wisdom is something that he holds apart from God, as did Adam who stands as the shadow behind him. The text of Genesis is implicit throughout Ezekiel.[23] The royal purple mantle of Tyre is ultimately draped over the concupiscent Great Whore of Revelation, an emblem of regal complicity with worldly sin.

The beauty of the King of Tyre is the scriptural source for the tradition that ascribes beauty to Lucifer. A beauty temporary and illusory. The sixteenth century *Livre des Esperitz* bears testimony to the persistence of the tradition in the grimoires:[24]

> Lucifer was very beautiful and of like status to the other good angels, but he did not dwell in the heavens for more than the space of an hour, for he became proud looking at and contemplating the great beauty in which he had been formed; and all others that conspired with him were thrown into Hell in confusion. And as for Lucifer, according to the doctors of nigromancy, said Lucifer presides in Hell and all the aforesaid spirits of Hell obey him as the lord of Hell.

The Principate of Fallen Angels

The Principate of Fallen Angels is a spirit catalogue that comprises
the twenty angels of 1 Enoch. As noted, the orthography is that of
the definitive work of Vanderkam and Black, which replaces the
previous standard work of Charles. As a result, it has been possible to
ascribe accurate gematria values to them. The powers are extracted
from those names which suggest functions, and in the case of the
superiors Šemhazah (1) and Asa'el (10) is supplemented with the
information related in the text of 1 Enoch.

From these bare bones it is possible to engage in the speculative
art of conjuring. Though no working method can be surmised from
the list, it is not without precedent. The grimoire tradition is characterised by such spirit lists, with practitioners using the operating
procedure of their choice. In the case of the *Lemegeton*, the appended system is essentially that of the *Heptameron*. All the grimoires
draw on an inheritance of exorcism manuals – and notable in this
respect is the *Grimorium Verum* – the key procedure of which is the
attainment of the spirit signature, or seal. Most commonly in Europe
magicians have turned to the *Key of Solomon* to find their armorium.
It is Solomon who is the great patron of the art, and his *Testament*
provides one method by which the spirits may be summoned. The

Testament should be consulted as our earliest example of the tradition, even if we ultimately apply other means, or draw inspiration from late texts such as the *Grand Grimoire* or *Dragon Rouge*. The art of conjuring is personal, though patterned on clear principles that are our unbroken magical tradition. My approach will be outlined in the subsequent volume, *Praxis*. For the already proficient magician, the spirit list alone will suffice, though there is always benefit in comparative study.

In the *Principate* it is apparent that Šemhazah and Asa'el are superiors, and as I have argued, derived from different traditions. As such, they deserve closer attention. Though the Judaic understanding of Šemhazah is 'God seeth,' Martin Noth proposes that the name (ŠM) refers to the Phoenician healer god of Sidon, Ešmun whom is later syncretised with Asclepius. Ešmun is appropriately a beautiful youth, the young god archetype to which Lucifer also inheres. Šemhazah is eventually eclipsed in favour of Azazel who becomes the proto Belial/Satan figure. The relationship of Asa'el/Azazel needs elucidation. The Asa'el of 1 Enoch 8 is rendered as Azazel elsewhere in the text. The more common Azazel becomes the accepted orthography, no doubt aided by the scapegoat of Leviticus who suffers an identical fate. The etymology of 'strong god' is apt for a rival to Yahweh. Following this arc, Lucifer and Satan replace Šemhazah/Azazel as the names, or titles, of choice.

The powers of the angels in the Principate are indicated by their names. These are largely divinatory and astral, preoccupations which hark back to Mesopotamia, as discussed in reference to the Apkallu. Dan'el however is Canaanite,[1] included conceivably because he is a follower of Rpu-B'l, the leader of the Rephaim. The fragmentary CTA 20–22 has been proposed as evidence that Dan'el descended to the underworld and encountered the Rephaim in the desire to bring his precious son back to life. Dan'el is invoked in Ezekiel 28:3 as part of the curse against the King of Tyre, 'Behold, thou art wiser than Daniel; there is no secret that they can hide from thee.' Note the Orphic character of Dan'el's underworld quest, and its allied sapiential motif.

Analysis of the names shows Phoenician, Canaanite and Mesopotamian genealogies. The fallen angels are healers, the Mighty Dead and wisdom teachers, whose theophanies as the wild elemental powers may point to older shamanic, and arguably paleolithic, survivals. Such manifestations provide a bridge that enables us to reestablish contact.

Some of these angels appear to have passed into the magical tradition, but direct identification is to be cautioned against. Kokab, for example, is the generic 'star' and can as easily refer to Venus as Mercury; the sense in which Kokabiel is encountered in Kabbalistic magic. Black and VanderKam suggest a connection with the Hêlêl Ben Šaḥar of Isaiah for Kokab'el, though it seems a stretch given the extensive commentary I have provided on the origins of this 'name.'

It is intriguing and instructive that the powers of the spirits in the Principate – namely divination, craft skills, seduction, metallurgy, spell-binding and breaking, herb and plant lore, semiotics, rhetoric, astrology/astronomy and weather magic – have direct parallels in the grimoires, whose spirits are explicitly identified as the fallen angels. Riddling the ashes does not result in exact matches spirit to spirit, nor should that be expected. The grimoires are the repositories of the Western magical tradition, the result of a flow of information, technologies and stories between cultures.

Fundamentally, the fallen angels cannot be categorised as evil, but are rival deities in an ongoing process of demonisation. They are of an entirely different class of entity to the disease demons which exorcism customarily deals with. Neither are they the powers of darkness, though that is how they are often presented. Magic and witchcraft have preserved not the letter, but the spirit of this, with the understanding of the necessity of intercourse with wisdom teachers. The fount and figurehead of this confluence of traditions now bears the name of Lucifer.

	ANGEL	ARAMAIC	GEMATRIA	MEANING
1	Šemhazah	שׁמיחזה	370	*N.N. (God) Seeth*
2	Arteqif*	ארעתקף	851	*The Earth is Power*
3	Ramt'el*	רעטאל	280	*Burning Ashes of El*
4	Kokab'el	כוכבאל	79	*Star of El*
5	Ur'el	אוריאל	248	*Fire/Light of El*
6	Ram'el*	רעמאל	341	*Thunder of El*
7	Dan'el	דניאל	95	*El is Judge*
8	Ziq'el	זיקאל	148	*Fireball of El*
9	Baraq'el	ברקאל	333	*Lightning of El*
10	Asa'el	עסאל	161	*El has Made*
11	Hermoni	חרמוני	314	*Of Hermon*
12	Matr'el	מטראל	280	*Rain of El*
13	Anan'el	עננאל	201	*Cloud of El**
14	Sithwa'el*	סיתואל	507	*Winter of El**
15	Šims'el	שמשיאל	681	*Sun of El*
16	Šahr'el	שהריאל	546	*Moon of El*
17	Tamm'el	תמיאל	481	*El has Completed*
18	Tur'el	טוראל	246	*Mountain of El*
19	Yamm'el	יעיאל	91	*Sea of El*
20	Zehor'el	זהריאל	253	*Brightness of El*

* Entries marked with an asterisk are speculative or dispiuted.

POWER	OBSERVATION
Binding spells, cutting of roots	Alternative meaning: *The Name (N.N.) Rebel*
Auguries of the Earth	Presumably geomancy; also necromancy.
Volcanic activities*	See Caim, the 53rd spirit of the *Lemegeton*. Also Hephaestus and Tubal Cain.
Astral divination and semiotics*	Associated with Mercury in Kabbalistic magic
Pyromancy*	Uriel becomes an archangel, replacing the original Sariel.
Brontomancy*	Power given as 'true visions' in 2 Baruch 55:3
Dispensing justice, wisdom	Canaanite hero known from the *Epic of Aqhat*; also see Ezekiel 14:14–20 and 28:3.
Auguries of comets*	
Auguries of lightning	
Secrets of heaven, iniquities on Earth, weaponry, cosmetics, seduction	Becomes combined with the Azazel of Leviticus
Loosing spells, magic, sorcery, sophistry, rhetoric	See previous references to Mount Hermon
Rain making*	
Nephomancy*	
Auguries of the Sun	
Auguries of the Moon	
	Genesis 46:10, Exodus 6:15
	Ezekiel 8:2, Daniel 12:3

Endnotes

A HISTORY OF ERROR

1   Of particular interest here is Armando Maggi's *Satan's Rhetoric: A Study of Renaissance Demonology*, which shows how this concept was extended to an insane degree with supposed subtle emphasis of speech, for example in the recitation of psalms, adduced to be the interjection of Satanic ambiguity.
2   The key biblical texts for this are Gen. 1, Rev. 12, and Dan. 7. The combat myth is of use when considering the role of Satan as adversary, imagery in particular developed by Paul in Ephesians. The best study of this material, though not without isssues, is: Forsyth, 1987. *The Old Enemy*, Princeton.
3   Witzel, E.J. Michael, 2012. *The Origins of the World's Mythologies*. Oxford University Press. Thanks to Gordon White for drawing my attention to this important work.

THE DAWN BREAKERS

1   Dew here is equivalent to semen.
2   See, for instance, Oates, Shani, 2011. 'It's all in a Name: Lucifer, an Ancient Heresy.' *The Arcane Veil*. Mandrake of Oxford.
3   See Michael Howard and Nigel Jackson's reliance on Madeline Montalban as a primary source for their Lumiel/Lucifer/Christ hybrid in *The Pillars of Tubal-Cain*. Capall Bann, 2000.

1 Olmstead, 1908. *Western Asia in the Days of Sargon of Assyria*. New York: Henry Holt.

2 For more on this see Smith, Sidney, 1925. *The Cambridge Ancient History* (volume 3 of 12 vols.)

3 Olmstead, op. cit.

4 See the tablets K.3401, S.2118, K.4470 and No 47449.

5 As was Moses, see Exodus 2:1–10.

6 Smith, op. cit.

7 Ibid.

8 Though Venusian, we travel here in the opposite direction to Sargon on his pilgrimage to Cyprus.

9 Gunkel, H., 1895. *Schöpfung und Chaos in Urzeit and Endzeit*. Göttingen: Vandenhoeck und Ruprecht.

10 I have avoided delving into the debate over the differences between Canaanite, Ugaritic and Amorite. In this I take the position of Mark S. Smith in *The Origins of Biblical Monotheism*, where he states: 'No matter how this cultural relationship is resolved, the diversity of later reflexes of material in the Ugaritic texts shows that mythic narratives were transmitted in the areas known in the Bible as Canaan and Israel.' (Oxford: Oxford University Press, 2001.) My concern here is with this mythic narrative.

11 Wildberger, H. Jesaja, 1972. BKAT, 10.1; Neukirchen-Vluyn: Neukirchener Verlag.

12 Albright, W.F., 1968. *Yahweh and the Gods of Canaan: A Historical Analysis of Two Contrasting Faiths*. Doubleday and Company.

13 For more on Albright and his influence over biblical scholarship see Burke O. Long's comprehensive *Planting and Reaping Albright: Politics, Ideology, and Interpreting the Bible*. Pennsylvania State University Press, 1997.

14 A brilliant study on this is executed by Edward L. Greenstein in his paper 'The God of Israel and the Gods of Canaan: How different were they?' which concludes biblical scholarship is 'significantly influenced by theological and ideological interests.' *Proceedings of the World Congress of Jewish Studies*, 1997.

1   In the KTU, Zaphon as the dwelling place of Baal and the Mount of the Divine
    Assembly are differentiated. This is not the case in Isaiah 14:13, where the
    two are clearly conflated and confused.

2   See here Proverbs 25:23: the north wind brings forth rain, although this has
    been garbled in the KJV rendering.

3   See KTU 1.1 V 5; 1.6 VI 1–2, 12–13, 33–35.

4   Clifford, R., 1972. *The Cosmic Mountain in Canaan and the Old Testament*. Harvard
    University Press.

5   Parpola, Simo, 1999. 'Sons of God: The Ideology of Assyrian Kingship.' *Archae-
    ology Odyssey Archives*.

6   In the KJV translation sapphire is given, meaning blue stone.

7   It is of profit to compare this with Matthew 4:8.

8   For more on this see Robin Lane Fox, 2008. *Travelling Heroes: Greeks and their
    Myths in the Epic Age of Homer*. Penguin Books.

9   We may also add that the rising and setting of Venus as morning and evening
    star traces the shape of horns rising from each horizon.

10 The practically minded will note that elfshot are the European witchcraft
    version of such divine stones and can be venerated in Luciferian work as
    the house of the god (Beth-El).

11 A similar statement is found in Pliny's *Natural History*: 'Above (the City) Seleu-
    cia, there is another Mountain named Casius, as well as the other. This is of
    that Height, that if a Man be upon the Top of it in the Night, at the Fourth
    Watch, he may behold the Sun rising. So that with a little turning of his
    Body, he may at one Time see both Day and Night.' There is an intimation
    here of Parmenides' gates of Day and Night.

SCORCHED HEAVENS, BURNED EARTH

1   Gunkel, Hermann, 1895. *Creation and Chaos in the Primeval Era and the Eschaton*.
    (Trans. Whitney Jr., K.W.) William B. Eerdmans, Grand Rapids MI 2006.

2   Gruppe, Otto, 1906. *Griechische Mythologie und Relionsgeschichte*. Munich.

3   Grelot, P., 1953. 'Isaïe XIV 12–15 et son arriere-plan mythologique.' *RHR* 149,
    18–48.

4   Two passages are relevant: *Theogony* 378–382 and 986–991.

5   *The History of Herodotus* III:115.

6   The rising of the star of Eridu marking the end of the Summer drought. For the sake of accuracy we note that the star (*mul nun-ki*) and the Greek constellation do not coincide, but are separated in the heavens by Orion.

7   Giorgio de Santillana and Hertha von Dechend, 1969. *Hamlet's Mill: An Essay on Myth and the Frame of Time*. New Hampshire: David R. Godine.

8   Astour, 1967: 270.

9   *Euripides: Selected Fragmentary Plays*, Vol. 1. Edited with introductions, translations and commentaries by C. Collard, M.J. Cropp and K.H. Lee. Aris & Phillips Ltd., Warminster 1995.

10 The earliest reference is found in *Iliad* VI:156: 'to Bellerophontes the gods granted beauty and desirable manhood.' A couple of examples from grimoires: in the *Grimorium Verum*: Lucifer appears in the form and figure of a fair boy; and is said to be very beautiful in *Le Livre des Esperitz*. The remarked beauty of the King of Tyre, who will be considered in 'The Cloven Hoof,' should perhaps be regarded as correspondent, identifying him with the young god.

11 It is particularly associated with the 'dying' gods (Adonis et alii) and thus has strong fertility/healing/underworld connotations.

12 Ted Hughes' *Shakespeare and the Goddess of Complete Being* examines the same mythic structure – which he terms the tragic equation – as it is found in Shakespeare.

13 Detienne, M. & Vernant J-P., 1978. 'The Live Bit' *Cunning Intelligence in Greek Culture and Society*. Translated by Janet Lloyd, The Harvester Press, Sussex. Detienne, M. & Wirth, A.B., 'Athena and the Mastery of the Horse' in *History of Religions* vol. 11, no.2 (Nov. 1971): 161–184.

14 Astour, 1967: 225–228.

15 In a note to his text, Astour comments: 'It may be worthwhile to quote the pseudoepigraphic Testament of Solomon, according to which Solomon built temples to Baal and Raphan [...] Raphan is exactly the Ugaritic Rpan = Rap-a-na; there probably still was a healing-god of that name in Syria toward the end of the pre-Christian era.' Astour, 1967: 226.

16 Sumerian Muš (Serpent) was the son of Baal and Anat, who was also referred to as 'the little one.'

17 Astour, 1967: 265.

18 Kinnier Wilson, J.V., 1985. The Legend of Etana. Warminster: Aris and Phillips.

19 Etana, who ruled from the city of Kish, is recorded as being the thirteenth king, the first after the flood. Twelve prediluvian kings ruled before him.

20 Late Version, tablet II, lines 37–44.

1   Klaas Spronk, 'Down with Helel! The Assumed Mythological Background of
    Isa. 14:12,' in M. Dietrich, I. Kottsieper (Eds.), *Und Mose schrieb dieses Lied auf:
    Studien zum Alten Testament und zum Alten Orient* (Fs O. Loretz; AOAT 250),
    Münster 1998, 717–726.

2   Prinsloo, W. S., 1981. 'Isaiah 14:12-15: Humiliation, Hubris, Humiliation'
    Zeitschrift für die alttestamentliche Wissenshaft 93: 436.

3   Saints here is a translation for angels, being the same as the 'sons of god' or as-
    tral powers of the *bene 'elohim* of Genesis 6:1–4; lines that will require further
    exegesis when we discuss the Enochian tradition in chapter 13.

4   Shipp, R. Mark, 2003.

5   Canaanite and Ugaritic must also be considered carefully.

6   Saint Giuseppe Moscati (1880–1927), a Neapolitan doctor, belongs to this same
    tradition, and to this day is said to keep office hours and prescribe from
    beyond the grave.

7   Pitard, Wayne T., 1999. 'The Rpum Texts.' *The Handbook of Ugaritic Studies.*
    Edited by Watson, Vyatt. Leiden: Brill.

8   In the same way one works with an ancestor shrine and tends the local grave-
    yard.

9   The current trend of eschewing compulsion in spirit work is out of character
    with all previous shamanic practice, though this is precisely what the exor-
    cism texts the grimoires are modelled on has preserved.

10 See Hosea 6:1–3 for a biblical account of this ritual.

11 Dietrich, M., Loretz, O., & Sanmartín, J., 1976. KTU² Teil 1: Transkription,
    AOAT 24/1. Kevelaer and Neukirchen-Vluyn.

12 On this, see Astour, (1967): footnote 4 (190), in which he considers the note-
    worthy suggestion by Schultze (1876) that the second part of the name of
    Dionysus can be etymologically related to the Hebrew *nēs*, meaning 'stake'
    or 'pole.'

13 This gives us insight into the deeper symbolism of the threshing floor in the
    Enochian eschatology of Kelley and Dee. The threshing floor is also the site
    of the Temple of Solomon, see 2 Samuel 24 and 1 Chronicles 21:15.

14 Consider how the early Church hijacked and demonised Baal and the Rephaim,
    as the dying and resurrection of their saviour/healer god Jesus at Easter
    supplanted the cult of the earlier god. Note, furthermore, that the Autumn
    equinox is also given as the timing for the return of the Rephaim, in con-
    trast to the timing given by Spronk for the return of Baal and renewal of
    the king.

15   The combat myth is outside the scope of this study, and I only wish to inter-
pose it in passing. See Forsyth et al.

16   The descent of Inanna/Ištar encodes the Venus cycle.

17   Observe how this is played out in Revelation 21:23: 'And the city had no need
of the sun, neither of the moon, to shine in it: for the glory of God did
lighten it, and the Lamb is the light thereof.'

THE INVISIBLE GOD

1   Deuteronomy 7:2 gives the character of this annexation, 'when the Lord thy
God shall deliver them before thee; thou shalt smite them, and utterly
destroy them; thou shalt make no covenant with them, nor shew mercy
unto them.'

2   Compare this with the vision of Kelley and Dee, who saw the 24 elders of days,
but arrayed about an empty throne, in marked contrast with Revelation.
They were clearly influenced in this by the Deuteronomist view, not simply
the fear of being branded heretics.

3   See also 1 John 4:12 and 1 Timothy 6:16.

4   The division of the world beneath different stellar contingencies is notably
taken up in the work of Dee.

5   Kaufmann, Y., 1960. *The Religion of Israel, from Its Beginnings to the Babylonian
Exile.* University of Chicago Press.

6   Green, Alberto R.W., 2003. *The Storm God in the Ancient Near East.* University of
California Press.

7   Judges 21:25, 'In those days there was no king in Israel: every man did that
which was right in his own eyes.'

8   See also the account of the rite in Numbers 29 and Isaiah 53.

9   Evangelical Christians often use the cessation of the thread turning white in
the atonement ritual as evidence that Judaism and animal sacrifice have
been superseded by the sacrifice of the Christ.

10   'For the highest spiritual working one must accordingly choose that victim
which contains the greatest and purest force. A male child of perfect in-
nocence and high intelligence is the most satisfactory and suitable victim.'
Aleister Crowley, *Magick in Theory and Practice*, Chapter XII 'Of the Bloody
Sacrifice: and Matters Cognate'

1   Blair, Judit M., 2009. *De-demonising the Old Testament: An Investigation of Azazel, Lilith, Deber, Qeteb and Reshef in the Hebrew Bible*. Tübingen: Mohr.

2   Tawil, Hayim, 1980. 'Azazel the Prince of the Steepe: A Comparative Study.' *ZAW* 92: 43–59.

3   Observe that the woven crown is a spirit trap, still an important demonological tool.

4   Often translated incorrectly, but to the delight of schoolboys, as haemorrhoids.

5   See Lecouteux, Claude, 2003. *Witches, Werewolves and Fairies: Shapeshifters and Astral Doubles in the Middle Ages*. Inner Traditions.

6   Agrippa, *Three Books of Occult Philosophy*, Book I, ch. 24 'What things are lunary, or under the power of the Moon.'

7   Kelley must surely have been aware of these passages: 'Babalon' is translated as 'wicked' and 'Babalond' as 'harlot.'

8   This connection is often forgotten in favour of Pan, the beloved image of wild nature in the Romantic period.

THE SERPENT IN THE GARDEN

1   Respectively found in Genesis (see also 3 Baruch), Leviticus and Ezekiel. Isaiah gives no description beyond shining, this quality is the origin of 2 Corinthians 11:14, 'And no marvel; for Satan himself is transformed into an angel of light.'

2   In another sense the Devil represents bondage to our desires, and the material world, as exhibited in the tableau of Le Diable in the Tarot de Marseille.

3   *Panarion* is the Greek for medicine chest, in that the book details heresies and the Christian antidotes for them. The text is also known as *Adversus Haereses*, and his work informed Augustine's similarly monickered *Against all Heresies*.

4   *Panarion*, Book I, chapter XXXVII, 2, 5.

5   *Panarion*, Book I, chapter XXXVII, 5, 3–8.

6   It is not the Cain who kills Abel who is linked with witchcraft, this distinction goes to Cain (also Cainan), son of Arp'ak'sad, of whom it is said in the Syrian tradition: 'It was this Cain who increased the deviation of the Chaldeans, witchcraft and divination by the stars. His descendants worshipped him as a god and erected a statue of him during his lifetime.

This became the beginning of idol worship. [Cain] built a city and named it Harran after his son.' The quotation comes from the *Chronicles of Michael the Syrian*, drawn from early sources, though contemporaneous with the Crusades and the Templars, whom he describes. If a witchcraft tradition did owe anything to this lineage we might expect it to have preserved the memory of these two Cains. Note also the connection to the founding of the city of Harran. From Green, 1992: '...Harran was notorious among Christians for the persistent practices of its ancient rites and cults well after the official victory of the Church.'

7   The sign was venerated by the Jews of Asia Minor, as the triple Digamma, equivalent to 666. It is very likely that John of Patmos knew this sign, and of its association with the lion-serpent.

8   For a full account of the gnostic gems see Mastrocinque, Attilio, 2005. *From Jewish Magic to Gnosticism*. Mohr Siebeck.

9   *Against Heresies* I 30,15

10 This is similar to the Nicolaitan heresy condemned in Revelation 2:6 and 2:14–15

11 For the white stone, see also Isaiah 56:5. Paradoxically, the methodology used by John to attain the visionary states of Revelation: incubation. For more on this see 'The Cup, the Cross and the Cave' in my *Apocalyptic Witchcraft*.

12 Justin Martyr, *First Apology*, Chapter 22.

13 Justin Martyr, *Dialogue with Trypho*, Chapter 69.

14 Origen, *Homily on Leviticus*, S.I.9

15 Tertullian, *Apology*, Chapter 22.

16 See the previous mention of Ningišzida.

17 Consider also the brazen serpent of Moses, whose own name is now accepted to derive from the Mesopotamian *muš*, meaning serpent, rather than any Egyptian etymology. The serpents of Eden and brass were indeed conflated in the heresies of the Ophites and Peratae.

18 Wilson, Leslie S., 2001.

19 Earlier I elucidated the identity of the king as tree, but so too are gods, goddesses, heroes and the watchers. The Middle Persian *Book of Giants* preserves this tradition in a fragment: 'and the trees that came out, those are the watchers, and the giants that came out of the women.'

20 The success of Barbara Black Koltuv's ahistorical but influential *The Book of Lilith* has somewhat eclipsed this fact; Eve is perhaps more worthy of attention than Lilith, whose legend appears very late in the c.7–10 CE *Alphabet of ben Sira*.

21 See Ted Hughes op. cit. for a dazzling exposition of this.

22 For Clement of Alexandria's identification of Eve with the Dionysisan 'Evoe!' see Astour, 1967: 193–4.

23 Though it has been suggested that *Malleus Maleficarum* has been over-empha-sised, there is no denying the pervading misogyny of the period.

24 According to Josephus, mandrake is more commonly דודי (*duday*) from the root for 'beloved.'

25 Josephus, The Wars of the Jews, Book VII, Chapter 6.3

26 Dated to 2450–2350 BCE, it predates the *Epic of Gilgameš*, the earliest version of which is the 'Old Babylonian' from the eighteenth century BCE. In fact, Gilgameš is the son of the union of Lugalbanda and Ninsun. I am indebted to the anonymous academic, whose talk at Treadwell's Bookshop on the Vernal Equinox 2014, brought my attention to the close connection, in this earliest of myths, between the sex magical rite, or *hieros gamos*, and the necromantic rite.

27 For the mountain (*kur*) as otherworldly topos, see *Apocalyptic Witchcraft*, and Alkistis Dimech, 'The Embodiment of Mystery' in *The Brazen Vessel*. The name of the goddess (Lady Wild Cow) can also be rendered Lamu-sumuna, the first part of which denotes a liminal, transforming, divine being.

28 'And he came to know a great light.' The light metaphor used in a sexual con-text is very unusual in Sumerian literature.

29 Peterson, J.H., 2001.

30 In the seal of Astaroth, the pentagram, or pentalpha, also symbolises the underworld, over which she is queen; the archaic association of the under-world and healing gods is remembered in the Pythagorean name for the pentagram: ὑγίεια (*hugieia*, health).

31 Whom Dee, not Crowley, first spelt as Babalon; the orthography that we use to make explicit that this is the revealed gnostic goddess and not a conven-tional biblical reading.

FALL AND FLOOD

1 By this I include the children of Genesis: Enoch, Jubilees, The Testaments of the Twelve Patriarchs et al.

2 See Witzel, E.J. Michael, 2012.

3 Students of the work of John Dee will recognise this phraseology from the Call of the Aethyrs.

4 See for instance Josephus, *Antiquities of the Jews*, Chapter 4.

5 See Numbers 13:33.

6   See 1 Enoch 6–11 and Jubilees 4–5.

7   That is, the etymology of both Nephilim and Jared.

8   In Kvanvig, 2011.

9   Bartelmus, R., 1979. *Heroentum in Israel und seiner Umwelt*. Theologische Verlag, Zurich; and Helge Kvanvig, 2011.

10   Ibid.

11   See Cain as founder of cities in Genesis 4:17

12   There is a grey area here, between ancestors, spirits, faery and ufonauts. What I mean specifically to exclude here is the 'nuts and bolts' technical explanation of civilisations and myths, not the entire realm of Magonia with which there is significant overlap.

13   Though this study focuses on the chthonic, Genesis is not primarily concerned with refuting the cultic underworld in the way that for example Isaiah does.

14   Wellhausen, J., 1957.

THE KEY

1   Witzel, E.J. Michael, 2012: 178–9.

2   A claim still repeated by those not au courant with the literature. For the original source of this see J.T. Milik, 1976. *Books of Enoch*. Oxford: Clarendon Press.

3   Though parallels with *Atra-Hasis* can be drawn, it is most likely that Genesis 6:2–4 is based on the lost *Phoenician History* of Philo of Byblos, combined with a mythical etiology for the origin of the great heroes among the primeval ancestors of the Canaanites, the *gibborim*, as divine beings residing in the netherworld. It is 1 Enoch, in its reading of Genesis 6:2–4, that presupposes *Atra-Hasis* in the sense that divine beings are the target of God's wrath.

4   Echoing the terms of Acéphale, I consider witchcraft to be a dismembered community.

5   Familiar to occultists from Joseph Freiherr von Hammer-Purgstall's imaginative interpretation of Baphomet as 'Bapho-Metis,' which he translates as Baptism of Fire. The Greek μῆτις (*mêtis*) is better translated as wisdom, craft or cunning. Originally she was a female Titan, the mother of Athene.

6   The existence of Göbekli Tepe has radically revised our understanding of the ability of hunter gatherers to act in unison. Previous wisdom insisted that the city/temple complex could not exist without agriculture. Another

potential example of this occurs in the *Chronicle* of Michael the Syrian, 1126–1199 CE; regarding the Tower of Babel, he writes: 'At the beginning of the days of Reu (R'awag) they commenced building the Tower in the Shenar country. Now the giant Nimrod hunted game for the builders and fed them.' Whilst acknowledging this, cities for the most part do require agriculture.

7 See the papers of Dr David Reich of the Harvard Medical School and Dr Benjamin Vernot and Dr Joshua Akey of the University of Washington.

8 There is a line drawn between us and the blood-drinkers whose savagery, not cooking the kill but devouring it raw, makes them less than human. See Lévi-Strauss, C., 1975. *The Raw and the Cooked: Introduction to a Science of Mythology*. Trans. John and Doreen Weightman. Harper Colophon Books; and also compare with the rites of Dionysus.

9 Finkelstein, J. J., 1958. 'Bible and Babel: A Comparative Study of Hebrew and Babylonian Religious Spirit.' *Essential Papers on Israel and the Ancient Near East*. Edited by Greenspahn, F. E., 1991. NY: New York University Press.

10 Noise is a defining characteristic of demonic incursion, whether for the desert anchorites, or in medieval demonology.

11 In the *Gilgameš* version of the *Atra-Hasis* narrative, he brings craftsmen (artificers) with him; and the animals laden onto the ark are wild rather than domesticated, which points to it preserving elements of early hunter-gatherer stories. See Finkel, Irving, 2014. *The Ark before Noah: Decoding the Story of the Flood*. Hodder and Stoughton.

12 An allusion worth bearing in mind when considering the name-as-slur Beelzebub.

13 This means contraception, for which the pomegranate is the enduring emblem. See Riddle, J. M., 1992 and 1997.

14 Federici, S., 2004. A reading that is indebted to Michel Foucault's understanding of the structure of power.

A MASS OF BLOOD AND FEATHERS

1 Another abridged source for 1 Enoch 1–7 is found in *The Chronicle of Michael the Great, Patriarch of the Syrians*.

2 And the desire, like Enoch, to encounter God through supreme piety; see Genesis 5:22–24.

3 Revelation is, of course, patterned on Daniel, so it is a text that remains required reading.

4   This phrase is of course the origin for *Liber AL vel Legis* 3:19 and witness to
     Crowley's own messianic pretensions. See 1 Maccabees 1:54, Daniel 9:27, 11.31
     and 12:11. The reference in Daniel is requoted in the synoptic gospels.

5   Collins, John Joseph, 1998. *The Apocalyptic Imagination: An Introduction to Jewish
     Apocalyptic Literature.* Wm. B. Eerdmans Publishing.

6   This was too late for John Dee (1527–1608), though he was keenly aware of the
     existence of the tradition.

7   See Milik, J. T., 1976.

8   For a comprehensive analysis of the text, see Stratton-Kent, 2014. *The Testa-
     ment of Cyprian the Mage.* Scarlet Imprint.

9   The combat myth and the Pauline conception of spiritual warfare have
     apocalyptic precursors, as does Revelation, relying as it does on Enoch and
     Daniel. In the fight against heresy and gnosticism the rebellion theme was
     inevitably amplified.

10   See, for example, Arnold, C. E., 1995.

11   For Mount Harmon as mountain of the Canaanite gods see Lipinski, E., 1971.
     'El's Abode. Mythological traditions related to Mount Hermon and to the
     mountains of Armenia.' *Orientalia Lovaniensia Periodica* 2. See also Psalm 68:
     the hill or mount of Bashan is properly Mount Harmon.

12   Karge, Paul, 1917. *Rephaim: Die vorgeschichtliche Kultur Palastinas und Phoniziens.*
     Paderborn. Translation author's own.

13   Though the enigmatic concentric rings of the Arabised Rogem Hiri, or to
     give it the modern Hebrew name Gilgal Rephaim (Wheel of Spirits), on the
     Golan Heights has been suggested. My preference is for the dolmen, as the
     tumulus at the centre of the enigmatic Gilgal Rephaim is not made from a
     single stone.

14   The ability to identify, connect with, and source power by working in sympa-
     thy with specific places is one way to define the practice of witchcraft.

15   In the military organisation of the era, a dekadarch/sergeant was in charge of
     a phalanx ten ranks deep. The use of battlefield language still points to a
     text composed in a time of war. Compare this with Mark 5:9: 'My name is
     Legion: for we are many.' A utilisation of Roman military terminology.

16   In 1 Enoch 68:4 an alternative name is offered: 'The name of the first is Yekun:
     he it was who seduced all the sons of the holy angels; and causing them to
     descend on earth, led astray the offspring of men.' The etymology of Yekun,
     once proposed as 'to rebel,' is now disputed.

17   A comparative study of the European grimoires also reveals the existence of
     variant older spirit lists.

18   Though known only to the Jewish people through secondary sources.

19 See the previously cited Lamentations 4:14-15.
20 See Blacker, Carmen, 1975. *The Catalpa Bow*. George Allen and Unwin.
21 See Eliade, M., 2004. *Shamanism*. Princeton University Press. Though reassessed, still a core text.
22 Stratton-Kent, J., 2010.
23 Nickelsburg, G.W.E., 1977. 'Apocalyptic and Myth in 1 Enoch 6-11.' *Journal of Biblical Literature* 96.
24 It is possible to argue that the inclusion of metalwork is a midrash on Tubal Cain, whom Genesis 4:22 describes as an 'artificer in brass and iron.' A designation used later for the fallen King of Tyre.
25 Thus, in ritual work, the use of these archangels at the quarters should be considered anathema, despite their pre-Judaic origins.
26 Compare 2 Peter 2:4-18, the other New Testament text drawn from the same source as the Epistle of Jude.
27 See the vision in Revelation 1:16, 20.
28 See Genesis 6:9: 'These are the generations of Noah: Noah was a just man and perfect in his generations, and Noah walked with God.'

CHILDREN OF ENOCH

1 Whilst noting that mentions of Satan/Satanail/Sotona in the Slavonic source, *Books of the Secrets of Enoch*, are now considered a fifteenth century revision.
2 VanderKam suggests the early Hasmonean 160-150 BCE, whilst Nickelsburg favours before the persecution of Antiochus Epiphanes (167 BCE) with Jubilees functioning as an anti-Hellenisation screed.
3 Known more commonly in the grimoires as Belial. He is the 68th spirit in the *Lemegeton*: 'created next after Lucifer and in the form of a beautiful angel, sitting in a chariot of fire, speaking with a comely voice declaring that he fell first & amongst the worthier and wiser sort which went before Michael & other heavenly angels.'
4 Here Cainan (also Cain), who we have already encountered; see 'The Serpent in the Garden,' note 6.
5 This can be compared with the way in which King Solomon is treated for his taking of foreign wives in 1 Kings 11.
6 The sin of Adam only becomes important in the first century CE in the writings of Paul, 4 Ezra and 2 Baruch.
7 Jubilees 15:26.

8   To argue otherwise would require significant evidence that has not to date
      been furnished. Suggestions that the Slavonic traditions were transmitted
      through the Bogomils or Cathars and entered into witchcraft traditions are
      an ahistorical pretension. Whilst it would be foolish to ignore the ongoing
      interest in angelology and apocalypse in monastic communities, there was
      certainly no unified witchcult within which such ideas could be preserved
      and circulated. Transmission via the Templars and thence Masonry is
      equally lacking in credibility.

9   See Orlov, Andrei A., 2009.

10   See 'Children of Enoch,' note 1.

11   A deliberate inclusion of a venus number, see also Mark 1:13. Indeed the whole
      of Mark 1 bears comparison with the themes of the *Apocalypse of Abraham*.

12   For the full list of forbidden birds, see Leviticus 11:13–19 and Deuteronomy
      14:12–18

13   [Abraham! And I said: Here I am thy servant. And he said: Know henceforth
      that the Eternal One hath chosen thee, He whom thou lovest; be of good
      courage and use this authority, so far as I bid thee, against him who slan-
      dereth truth; should I not be able to put him to shame who hath scattered
      over the earth the secrets of heaven and hath rebelled against the Mighty
      One?]
      [for thy heritage is to be over those existing without thee being born
      with the stars and clouds, with the men whose portion thou art, and who
      through thy being exist; and thine enmity is justification. On this account
      thy perdition disappear from me]

14   *City of God*, Book XV, Chapter 23.

15   It should be noted that this view is by no means exclusively Christian; the
      pagan world held similar beliefs.

16   See the *Panarion* of Epiphanius of Salamis 1: 9.3

17   Translated by Han J. W. Drijvers in Schneemelcher (ed.) *New Testament Apoc-
      rypha*, vol. 2, 380–385; Robert M. Grant, *Gnosticism*, 116–22; Bentley Layton,
      The Gnostic Scriptures: A New Translation with Annotations and Introductions,
      371–75; and Willis Barnstone in *The Gnostic Bible*, Shambhala 2003, 388–394.

18   These references are to be found in Tim. 73b ff., 91a ff.

19   Represented in the Hermetic tradition by the Tarot trump IX The Hermit,
      with his staff and lantern.

20   See McEvilley, Thomas, 1993.

21   A thorough, though not exhaustive, study of the history and significance of
      aiōn is Keizer, Heleen M., 2002. *Life-Time-Entirety. A Study of AIΩN in Greek
      Literature and Philosophy, the Septuagint and Philo*. Leiden: Brill.

22   Witzel, 2012: 367.
23   The rite of anointing associated with kingship is connected with replenishing
       the marrow, as are royal foods, such as honey. The Christian equivalent is
       the chrism.
24   See 'How in Modern Times Witches perform the Carnal Act with Incubus
       Devils, and how they are Multiplied by this Means' Sprenger and Kramer
       Malleus Maleficarum, London: Folio, 1968.
25   Drawing on Matthew 2:18 and the slaughter of the innocents by Herod.
26   See Cohn, N., 1975.

THE CLOVEN HOOF

1   See, for example, Mark 1:13.
2   Astour, 1967.
3   Though a disputed etymology, I defer to the standard reference work: Brown,
       River, Briggs, 1936. *A Hebrew and English Lexicon.* Oxford: Clarendon Press.
       Attempts to find a different etymology seem motivated by the desire to
       obscure the roots of Judaism in Canaanite religion.
4   For the New Testament teaching on this see Luke 11:34–35: 'The light of the
       body is the eye: therefore when thine eye is single, thy whole body also is
       full of light; but when thine eye is evil, thy body also is full of darkness.
       Take heed therefore that the light which is in thee be not darkness.'
5   It is an idea that persists in the grimoires, with an alternate name of Satan be-
       ing given as Mirage; and in the witch hunts, where the miracles of the Devil
       are dismissed as illusory. For 'Mirage,' see Kieckhefer, 1997. *Forbidden Rites:
       Necromancer's Manual of the Fifteenth Century.* Pennsylvania State University
       Press: 142–144.
6   See Cohn, N., 1975.
7   Kvanvig, H., 1988: 568.
8   Though a lost text, a fragment of the Book of Noah was incorporated into 1
       Enoch 106:2 and is the source of this quote.
9   See the smashed lamp symbolism in the record of Parsons and Hubbard's
       Babalon Working.
10   This emphasis was required by the Church Fathers to combat the Ophite and
       Naassene heresies that identified the Serpent in Eden as Christ.
11   Remembering that we have no 'Lucifer' until 382 CE.
12   For Leviathan see: Isaiah 27:1, Psalm 74:14, Psalm 104:26 and Job 41.
13   It is worth being familiar with the preceding Obadiah 3 for further context.

14 See the Song of Songs 2:14, and also Isaiah 2:19–21.

15 In Islam we discover Qaf (Kaf), the emerald mountain (or variously the emerald upon which the mountain is founded; or a range of encircling emerald mountains) which is said to be the abode of the djinn. The djinn are a race that predate Adam, and rebel, only to have their uprising quelled by Allah. Though the emerald mountain is remarkable, the other elements in the Qur'an seem to be derivative. The Qur'an is a relatively late text, revealed to Moḥammad over 609–632 AD and fixed in written form under the third caliph 'Utmān (Uthman) ibn 'Affān (644–656 AD). For this, and other, reasons, I have not felt it would be to my purpose to give an extended commentary on the Islamic material in this study.

16 Quoted from Walcot, P., 1978. *Envy and the Greeks*. Warminster: Aris & Phillips Ltd.

17 Compare this with Tertullian in *On the Apparel of Women*: 'And do you not know that you are each an Eve? The sentence of God on this sex of yours lives in this age: the guilt must of necessity live too. You are the devil's gateway: you are the unsealer of that forbidden tree: you are the first deserter of the divine law: you are she who persuaded him whom the devil was not valiant enough to attack...'

18 Theodoret of Cyrus, *Commentaire sur Isaie*, vol II, Sources Chrétiennes, Les Éditions du Cerf, 1980–1984.

19 Ibid.

20 Ibid.

21 Later it would serve a political purpose: the Catholic Church employed it as leverage against European monarchs to keep them in line.

22 Parpola, Simo, 1999. 'Sons of God: The Ideology of Assyrian Kingship' *Archaeology Odyssey Archives*.

23 A comprehensive survey of the Books of Adam and the meshing of the Watcher myth with that of Satan, which I have only touched upon, can be found in Neil Forsyth, *The Old Enemy*, Chapter 12.

24 'Le Livre des Esperitz' (The Book of Spirits). MS Cambridge, Trinity College O.8.29, folios 179–182vo. Translated by Alkistis Dimech.

APPENDIX: THE PRINCIPATE OF FALLEN ANGELS

1 See the *Epic of Aqhat*, CTA 17–19.

Bibliography

Aelian, (trans. Schofield, A. F. 1957). *De Natura Animalium*. Cambridge, MA: Harvard University Press.

Aeschylus. Translated by Smyth, Herbert Weir. Loeb Classical Library Volumes 145 & 146. Cambridge, MA: Harvard University Press. 1926.

Albani, Matthias, 2004. 'The Downfall of Helel the Son of Dawn: Aspects of Royal Ideology in Isa. 14:12-13.' Auffarth, Christoph, Stuckenbruck, Loren T. (eds.). *The Fall of the Angels. Themes in Biblical Narrative* 6. Leiden: Brill.

Albright, W.F., 1968. *Yahweh and the Gods of Canaan: A Historical Analysis of Two Contrasting Faiths*. Garden City, New York: Doubleday and Company.

Arnold, C. E., 1995. *The Colossian Syncretism*. Tübingen: Mohr Siebeck.

Astour, Michael C., 1967. *Hellenosemitica*. Leiden: Brill.

Barker, Margaret. 1987. *The Older Testament: The Survival of Themes from the Ancient Royal Cult in Sectarian Judaism and Early Christianity*. London: S.P.C.K.

Barnstone, William & Marvin Meyer, (eds.), 2003. *The Gnostic Bible*. Boston, Massachusetts: Shambhala.

Bartelmus, R., 1979. *Heroentum in Israel und seiner Umwelt*. Zurich: Theologische Verlag.

Baumgarten, Albert I., 1981. *The Phoenician History of Philo of Byblos: A Commentary*. Leiden: Brill.

Beer, G., 1900. 'Das Buch Henoch.' *Die Apokkyrphen und Pseudepigraphen des Alten Testaments*. Ed. E. Kautch. Tübingen: Mohr Siebeck (reprint 1921).

Bellemare, P.M., 1996. 'Meteorite Sparks A Cult.' *Journal of the Royal Astronomical Society of Canada* 90: 287.

Blacker, Carmen, 1975. *The Catalpa Bow*. London: George Allen & Unwin, 1975.

Blair, Judit, M,. 2009. *De-demonising the Old Testament: An Investigation of Azazel, Lilith, Deber, Qeteb and Reshef in the Hebrew Bible.* Tübingen: Mohr Siebeck.

Bodenheimer, F.S., 1960. *Animal and Man in Bible Lands.* Leiden: Brill.

Bordreuil, Pierre. 2007. 'Ugarit and the Bible: New Data from the House of Urtenu.' *Ugarit at Seventy-Five.* Lawson Younger Jr., K. (ed.). Eisenbrauns.

Boureau, Alain, 2006. *Satan the Heretic: The Birth of Demonology in the Medieval West.* Translated by Fagan, Teresa Lavander. Chicago/London: University of Chicago Press.

Box, G. H., (trans.), 1919. *The Apocalypse of Abraham.* London: S.P.C.K.

Brown, Francis, Driver, S. R., & Briggs, Charles A., 1936. *A Hebrew and English Lexicon.* Oxford: Clarendon Press.

Charlesworth, James H., 1983. *The Old Testament Pseudepigrapha, Volume One: Apocalyptic Literature and Testaments.* Peabody, Massachusetts: Hendrickson.

Clifford, R., 1972. *The Cosmic Mountain in Canaan and the Old Testament.* Cambridge, Mass.: Harvard University Press.

Clines, J.A., 1979. 'The Significance of the "Sons of God" Episode (Genesis 6:1–4) in the context of the 'Primeval History' (Genesis 1–11).' *Journal for the Study of the Old Testament* 13.

Collins, John Joseph, 1998. *The Apocalyptic Imagination: An introduction to Jewish Apocalyptic Literature.* Grand Rapids, MI: Wm. B. Eerdmans Publishing.

—— (ed.), 2000. *The Encyclopedia of Apocalypticism. Volume 1: The Origins of Apocalypticism in Judaism and Christainity.* New York/London: Continuum.

Cohn, Norman, 1975. *Europe's Inner Demons.* Brighton: Sussex University Press.

Day, J., 1985. *God's Conflict with the Dragon and the Sea: Echoes of a Canaanite Myth in the Old Testament.* Cambridge: University Press Cambridge.

Detienne, M. & Vernant J-P., 1978. 'The Live Bit.' *Cunning Intelligence in Greek Culture and Society.* Trans. by J. Lloyd. Sussex: The Harvester Press.

—— and Wirth, A.B., 1971. 'Athena and the Mastery of the Horse.' *History of Religions.* Vol. II, no. 2: 161–184.

Dietrich, M., Loretz, O., and Sanmartín, J., 1976. *Die Keilalphabetischen Texte aus Ugarit.* Teil 1: Transkription, AOAT 24/1. Kevelaer & Neukirchen-Vluyn.

Dimant, Devorah, 1978. '1 Enoch 6–11: A Methodological Perspective.' *Society of Biblical Literature 1978, Seminar Papers* Vol. 1, Missoula: Montana.

Dimech, Alkistis, (trans.), 2015. '*Le Livre des Esperitz*/The Book of Spirits.' *The Brazen Vessel.* London: Scarlet Imprint, 2019.

Drawnel, Henryk, 2012. 'Professional Skills of Asael (1 En. 8:1) and their Mesopotamian Background' 518–542. *Revue Biblique.* T. 119-4.

—— 2014. 'The Mesopotamian Background of the Enochic Giants and Evil Spirits.' 14–38. *Dead Sea Discoveries* 21. Leiden: Brill.

Eisenmann, Robert & Michael Wise, 1992. *The Dead Sea Scrolls Uncovered.* Rockport, MA: Element.

Eliade, Mircea, 2004. *Shamanism: Archaic Techniques of Ecstasy.* Princeton, NJ: Princeton University Press.

Faxneld, Per, 2013. *Satanic Feminism: Lucifer as the Liberator of Woman in Nineteenth Century Culture.* Stockholm: Molin and Sorgenfrei.

—— and Peterson, Jesper Aa., (eds.), 2013. *The Devil's Party: Satanism in Modernity.* Oxford: Oxford University Press.

Federici, S., 2004. *Caliban and the Witch: Women, the Body and Primitive Accumulation.* Brooklyn, NY: Autonomedia.

Finkel, Irving, 2014. *The Ark before Noah: Decoding the Story of the Flood.* London: Hodder and Stoughton.

Fox, Robin Lane, 2008. *Travelling Heroes: Greeks and their Myths in the Epic Age of Homer.* London: Penguin.

Freedman, David Noel (ed.), 1992. *The Anchor Bible Dictionary.* New York: Doubleday.

Frymer-Kensky, Tiva, 1977. 'The Atrahasis Epic and its Significance for our Understanding of Genesis 1-9.' *The Biblical Archaeologist* 40. no. 4.

Gordon, Cyrus Herzl, 1962. *Before the Bible: The Common Background of Greek and Hebrew Civilisation.* New York: Harper and Row.

Green, Alberto R. W., 2003. *The Storm-God in the Ancient Near East.* Winona Lake, Indiana: University of California.

Green, Tamara M., 1992. *The City of the Moon God: Religious Traditions of Harran.* Leiden: Brill.

Greenstein, Edward L., 1997. 'The God of Israel and the Gods of Canaan: How different were they?' *Proceedings of the World Congress of Jewish Studies/Division A: The Bible and its World*: 47-58. Margolin R. (ed.). World Union of Jewish Studies.

Grey, Peter, 2013. *Apocalyptic Witchcraft.* London: Scarlet Imprint.

Gunkel, Hermann, 1895. *Schöpfung und Chaos in Urzeit und Endzeit.* Göttingen: Vandenhoeck und Ruprecht.

Hannah, Darrell D., 1999. *Michael and Christ: Michael Traditions and Angel Christology in early Christianity.* Tübingen: Mohr Siebeck.

Hanson, P.D., 1977. 'Rebellion in Heaven and Euhemeristic Heroes in 1 Enoch 6-11.' *Journal of Biblical Literature* 96: 195-233.

—— 1979. *The Dawn of Apocalyptic: The Historical and Sociological Roots of Jewish Apocalyptic Eschatology.* Philadelphia: Fortress Press.

Hendel, Ronald S., 1987. 'Of Demigods and the Deluge: Toward an Interpretation of Genesis 6:1-4.' *Journal of Biblical Literature* 106, no. 1 (Mar., 1987): 13-26.

Hvidberg-Hansen, Finn Ove, 2007. 'Arṣû and 'Azîzû: A Study of the West Semitic "Dioscuri" and the Gods of Dawn and Dusk. Copenhagen: The Royal Danish Academy of Sciences and Letters.

Johannes, G., 2003. Theological Dictionary of the Old Testament: Volume 12. Translated by Green, David E. and Stott, Douglas W. Grand Rapids, Michigan: Eerdmans Publishing Company.

Kaufmann, Y., 1960. The Religion of Israel: From its Beginnings to the Babylonian Exile. Chicago: University of Chicago Press.

Karge, Paul, 1917. Rephaim: Die vorgeschichtliche Kultur Palastinas und Phoniziens. Ferdinand Schöningh: Paderborn. (Translated passage: Peter Grey)

Keizer, Heleen M., 2002. Life-Time-Entirety. A Study of ΑΙΩΝ in Greek Literature and Philosophy, the Septuagint and Philo. Leiden: Brill.

Kieckhefer, 1997. Forbidden Rites: A Necromancer's Manual of the Fifteenth Century: A Necromancer's Manual of the Fifteenth Century. Pennsylvania: Pennsylvania State University Press.

King, L.W. (ed.), 1907. Chronicles Concerning Early Babylonian Kings. Volume 2: Studies in Eastern History. London: Luzac and Co.

Koltuv, Barbara Black, 1986. The Book of Lilith. Lake Worth, FL: Nicholas-Hays.

Kramer, Heinrich & James Sprenger (trans. Montague Summers), 1968. Malleus Maleficarum. London: Folio Society.

Kvanvig, Helge S., 1988. Roots of Apocalyptic: The Mesopotamian Background of the Enoch Figure and of the Son of Man. Neukirchen-Vluyn: Neukirchener Verlag.

—— 2011. Primeval History: Babylonian, Biblical and Enochic: An Intertextual Reading. Leiden: Brill.

L'Heureux, Conrad, 1974. 'The Ugaritic and Biblical Rephaim.' The Harvard Theological Review 67, No. 3 (July): 265-274. Cambridge, MA.

Laessoe, J., 1956. 'The Atrahasis Epic: A Babylonian History of Mankind.' Bibliotheca Orientalis 13: 90-102.

Lamb, W.R.M., (Trans.), 1925. Plato in Twelve Volumes: Vol. 9. Cambridge, MA: Harvard University Press.

Lambert, W.G. and Millard, A.R., 1965. Cuneiform Texts from Babylonian Tablets in the British Museum: 46. London: British Museum.

Landau, Rom, 2008. Islam and the Arabs. Abingdon, Oxon: Routledge.

Lawlor, H.J. 1897. 'Early Citations from the Book of Enoch.' Journal of Philology 25: 164-225.

Levine, A. Baruch and Jean-Michel de Tarragon, 1984. 'Dead Kings and Rephaim: the Patrons of the Ugaritic Dynasty.' Journal of the American Oriental Society 104, no. 4 (Oct.-Dec.). American Oriental Society.

Lévi-Strauss, C., 1975. *The Raw and the Cooked: Introduction to a Science of Mythology*. Trans. by Weightman, John and Doreen. New York: Harper Colophon Books.

Lewis, Theodore J., 1996. 'CT 13.33–34 and Ezekiel 32: Lion-Dragon Myths.' *Journal of the American Oriental Society* 116: 28–47.

Lipinski, E., 1971. 'El's Abode: Mythological Traditions related to Mount Hermon and to the Mountains of Armenia.' *Orientalia Lovaniensia Periodica* 2: 15–41.

Long, Burke O., 1997. *Planting and Reaping Albright: Politics, Ideology and Interpreting the Bible*. Unversity Park: Pennsylvania University Press.

Manley, Johanna, 1995. *Isaiah Through the Ages*. Menlo Park, California: Monastery Books.

Mastrocinque, Attilio, 2005. *From Jewish Magic to Gnosticism*. Tübingen: Mohr Siebeck.

—— 2011. *Kronos, Shiva and Asklepios: Studies in Magical Gems and Religions of the Roman Empire*. Philadelphia: American Philosophical Society.

McEvilley, Thomas, 1993. 'The Spinal Serpent.' *RES: Anthropology and Aesthetics* 24: 67–77. Santa Monica, CA: The Getty Center for the History of Art and the Humanities.

Milik, J. T., 1976. *The Books of Enoch: Aramaic Fragments of Qumrân Cave 4*. Oxford: Oxford University Press.

Millard, A. R., 1967. 'A New Babylonian "Genesis" Story.' *TynBul* 18: 3–18.

Monroe, Lauren, 2012. 'Phinehas' Zeal and the Death of Cozbi: Unearthing a Human Scapegoat tradition in Numbers 25:1'18.' *Vetus Testamentum* 62: 211–231. Leiden: Brill.

Nickelsburg, G. W. E., 1977. 'Apocalyptic and Myth in 1 Enoch 6–11.' *Journal of Biblical Literature* 96.

Oates, Shani, 2011. *The Arcane Veil*. Oxford, UK: Mandrake of Oxford.

Olmstead, A. T., 1908. *Western Asia in the Days of Sargon of Assyria*. New York: Henry Holt.

Onians, R. B., 1988. *The Origins of European Thought*. Cambridge: Cambridge University Press.

Orlov, Andrei A., 2009. *Selected Studies in the Slavonic Pseudepigrapha*. Leiden: Brill.

—— & Gabriele Boccaccini (eds.), 2012. *New Perspectives on 2 Enoch: No Longer Slavonic Only*. Leiden: Brill.

Pagels, Elaine, 1995. *The Origin of Satan*. New York: Random House.

Parpola, Simo, 1999. 'Sons of God: The Ideology of Assyrian Kingship.' *Archaeology Odyssey* 2/5 (1999): 16–27.

Perrin, Bernadotte (trans.), 1921. *Plutarch's Lives*. London: W. Heinemann Ltd.

Peterson, Joseph H., 2001. *The Lesser Key of Solomon*. York Beach, ME: Weiser Books.

Pinker, Aron, 2007. 'A Goat to Go to Azazel.' *Journal of Hebrew Scriptures 7*, Article 8.

Pitard, Wayne T., 1999. 'The RpumTexts.' *Handbook of Ugaritic Studies*. Ed. Watson, Vyatt. Leiden: Brill.

Reed, Annette Y., 2005. *Fallen Angels and the History of Judaism and Christianity: The Reception of Enochic Literature*. Cambridge: Cambridge University.

Riddle, John M., 1992. *Contraception and Abortion from the Ancient World to the Renaissance*. Cambridge, Massachusetts/London, UK: Harvard University Press.

—— 1997. *Eve's Herbs: A History of Contraception and Abortion in the West*. Cambridge, Massachusetts/London, UK: Harvard University Press.

Schwartz, Howard, 1994. *Tree of Souls: The Mythology of Judaism*. Oxford: Oxford University Press.

Shipp, R. Mark, 2003. *Of Dead Kings and Dirges: Myth and Meaning in Isaiah 14:4b-21*. Leiden: Brill.

Smith, Mark S., 2001. *The Origins of Biblical Monotheism: Israel's Polytheistic Background and the Ugaritic Texts*. Oxford: Oxford University Press.

—— 2006. *The Rituals and Myths of the Feast of the Goodly Gods of KTU/CAT 1.23: Royal Constructions of Opposition, Intersection, Integration and Domination*. Atlanta: Society of Biblical Literature.

—— 2007. 'Recent Study of Israelite Religion in Light of the Ugaritic Texts.' *Ugarit at Seventy-Five*: 1–26. Lawson Younger Jr., K. (ed). Eisenbrauns.

Smith, Sidney, 1925. *The Cambridge Ancient History*. (vol. 3 of 12). Cambridge: Cambridge University Press.

Spronk, Klaas, 1986. *Beatific Afterlife in Ancient Israel and in the Near Ancient East*. Kevelaer: Butzon & Bercker; Neukirchen-Vluyn: Neukirchener Verlag.

—— 1998. 'Down with Helel! The Assumed Mythological Background of Isa. 14:12.' In M. Dietrich, I. Kottsieper (eds.), *'Und Mose schrieb dieses Lied auf': Studien zum Alten Testament und zum Alten Orient*. Fs O. Loretz; AOAT 250: 717–726. Münster: Ugarit Verlag.

Stoyanov, Yuri, 1994. *The Hidden Tradition in Europe*. London: Arkana.

—— 2000. *The Other God: Dualist Religions from Antiquity to the Cathar Heresy*. New Haven, CT: Yale University Press.

Stratton-Kent, Jake, 2009. *The True Grimoire*. London: Scarlet Imprint.

—— 2010. *Geosophia: The Argo of Magic*. London: Scarlet Imprint.

—— 2014. *The Testament of Cyprian the Mage*. London: Scarlet Imprint.

Stuckey, Johanna H. 2003. 'The Great Goddesses of the Levant.' *Journal of the Society for the Study of Egyptian Antiquities* 30: 127–157.

Sugg, Richard, 2013. *The Secret History of the Soul: Physiology, Magic and Spirit Forces from Homer to St Paul.* Newcastle upon Tyne: Cambridge Scholars.

Tawil, Hayim, 1980. 'Azazel the Prince of the Steepe: A Comparative Study.' *Zeitschrift für die Alttestamentliche Wissenschaft* 92 (1): 43–59.

Theodoret of Cyrus, (1980–1984). *Commentaire Sur Isaie. Vol II: Sources Chrétiennes.* Paris: Les Éditions du Cerf.

Toorn, K. van der, Bob Becking, Pieter Willem van der Horst (eds.), 1999 (second edition). *Dictionary of Deities and Demons in the Bible.* Leiden/Boston/Koln: Brill/Wm. B. Eerdmans Publishing.

VanderKam, James C., 1993. 'Biblical Interpretation in 1 Enoch and Jubilees.' *Journal for the Study of the Pseudepigrapha Supplement Series 14/Studies in Early Judaism and Christianity* 2: 96–125. Ed. J. H. Charlesworth and C. A. Evans. Sheffield: Sheffield Academic Press.

Walcot, Peter, 1978. *Envy and the Greeks.* Warminster, England: Aris and Phillips Ltd.

Watson, G. E. Wilfred and Nicholas Wyatt (eds.), 1999. *Handbook of Ugaritic Studies.* Leiden: Brill.

Wellhausen, J., 1957. *Prolegomena to the History of Ancient Israel.* New York: Meridian. (Originally published 1885)

Wilby, E., 2010. *The Visions of Isobel Gowdie: Magic, Witchcraft and Dark Shamanism in Seventeenth-Century Scotland.* Brighton: Sussex Academic Press.

Wildberger, H., 1980. *Jesaja.* Biblischer Kommentar Altes Testament 10.1. Neukirchen-Vluyn: Neukirchener Verlag.

Williams, Frank, (trans.), 1987. *The Panarion of Epiphanius of Salamis Book I* (Sects 1–146). De Fide. Leiden: Brill.

—— (trans.), 2013. *The Panarion of Epiphanius of Salamis Books II and III.* De Fide. Leiden: Brill.

Wilson, Leslie S. 2001. *The Serpent Symbol in the Ancient Near East: Nahash and Asherah, Death, Life, and Healing.* Lanham MD: University Press of America.

Witzel, E. J. Michael, 2012. *The Origins of the World's Mythologies.* New York: Oxford University Press.

Wyatt, N., 2002. *Religious Texts from Ugarit.* London: Sheffield University Press.

Young, Gordon Douglas (ed.), 1981. *Ugarit in Retrospect: Fifty Years of Ugarit and Ugaritic.* Winona Lake, Indiana: Eisenbrauns.

Index

201

Philo of Byblos 92, 186, 190, 196
Philtron 39
Pingala 147, 148
Plant knowledge 39, 173
Plato 37, 147, 196
   Timaeus 37, 147
Pliny 149, 179
Plutarch 149, 198
Process Church of the Final Judgment 17
Prometheus 35, 101, 117, 123
Psalms 22, 60, 167
   Psalm 48 28
   Psalm 82 90
   Psalm 109 (KJV 110) 14, 15, 17
Psellus, Michael 47, 135
   On the Work of Demons 47
Pyramid texts 51
Pythagorean tradition 147

Q
Qaf 192
Qudšu 80
Qumran 8, 66, 107, 108, 129, 132, 158
Qur'an 134, 163, 192

R
Raphan 180
Rebellion 3, 4, 5, 26, 38, 64, 69, 72, 92, 93, 96, 98, 99, 101, 102, 109, 111, 113, 132, 157, 158, 188, 195
Rephaim 39, 45, 46, 47, 48, 49, 50, 51, 79, 92, 94, 111, 112, 132, 136, 157, 163, 172, 181, 196
Revelation 4, 6, 7, 8, 16, 21, 29, 30, 34, 36, 37, 50, 58, 60, 67, 69, 73, 74, 76, 79, 84, 86, 118, 122, 123, 127, 138, 143, 144, 150, 155, 159, 160, 161, 168, 182, 184, 187, 188, 189
Rpu-B'l 39, 172

S
Sabbat 63, 72, 73, 96, 115, 152
Sacrifice 3, 32, 48, 49, 50, 60, 61, 62, 64,
65, 68, 69, 73, 79, 98, 101, 131, 136, 182
Samael 73, 80, 156, 166
Sargon I 19, 20
Sargon II 19, 21, 31, 48, 53
Satan 16, 17, 18, 43, 44, 45, 76, 78, 79, 84, 90, 91, 103, 122, 123, 129, 131, 132, 133, 134, 135, 142, 155, 156, 157, 158, 159, 160, 161, 162, 163, 164, 165, 166, 167, 168, 172, 177, 183, 189, 191, 192, 194, 197
Satanail 134, 135, 189
Scapegoat 61, 62, 64, 68, 121, 155, 156, 172
Second Temple 53, 60, 61, 104, 157
Sefer Hekhalot 135
Seirim 65, 70
Seleucus the Diadochan 31, 32
Semen 96, 146, 147, 149, 151, 152
Šemhazah 110, 113, 116, 117, 119, 124, 126, 132, 134, 171, 172
Septuagint 13, 21, 64, 190, 196
Serpent 24, 27, 31, 39, 41, 46, 71, 72, 73, 74, 75, 76, 79, 80, 81, 82, 83, 84, 100, 109, 115, 122, 123, 132, 134, 139, 142, 146, 147, 148, 149, 158, 161, 163, 164, 165, 167, 180, 184
Sex magic 120, 141, 150
Shakespeare 149, 150, 180
Shamanism 63, 96, 117, 127
Sheol 36, 41, 45, 92, 157
Simon Magus 142, 147, 168
Sirius 51, 52, 82
Solomon 2, 59, 60, 79, 81, 82, 108, 132, 144, 168, 171, 180, 181, 189, 198
   Song of Songs 65, 82, 192
Sons of God 86, 87, 88, 179, 192, 194, 197
Sophia 75, 145
Sparagmos 96
Spinal serpent 148
Spronk, Klaas 42, 48, 181, 198
Stang 48
Stellar wisdom 43, 151, 152
Stones 10, 11, 31, 33, 74, 116, 143, 144, 145, 146
Sumer 20, 40

9 780957 449244